Rest & Be Restored
He is your Righteousness
and you are new in
Him 2 COR 5:17
Blessings
Rick Sarver

I'm Saved. Now What?

Learn key truths that will help you experience abundant life.

Rick Sarver

I'M SAVED. NOW WHAT?

Copyright © December 2014 by Rick Sarver

Published by Freedom Place Publishing
A Division of Freedom Ministries International
Myrtle Beach, SC
www.fmintl.org

Permission is granted to copy this publication in whole or in part but not for sale or profit provided that this copyright and limited permission to copy is included in all copies.

The Bible text used in this publication is the King James Version unless otherwise noted.

Cover Design: Kimberly T. Riley
Prepared for Publication: Dr. Lonnie E. Riley

ISBN-13:
978-1505610710

ISBN-10:
1505610710

Printed in the United States

DEDICATION

I dedicate this book to my mom, Dixie Lee Jordan. You have been such an inspiration to me. You have been such a great example of a victorious Christian.

Thank you for praying for me and always believing in me through the good and the bad. Without your love and prayers I would not have been able to write this book. I am so blessed to have you as my mom.

CONTENTS

- DEDICATION 5
- FOREWORD 9
- REPENT! 13
- BELIEVING THE RIGHT GOSPEL 21
- NO MORE CONDEMNATION! 31
- SELF RIGHTEOUSNESS OR FAITH RIGHTEOUSNESS? ... 37
- AWAKE TO RIGHTEOUSNESS 53
- THE BORN IDENTITY 71
- THE KEY TO VICTORIOUS LIVING 79
- FREE TO BE YOU 85
- FROM THE LAW WAY TO THE GRACE WAY 93
- THE KINGDOM OF GOD AND GRACE 101
- THE KINGDOM OF GOD AND GRACE 2 115
- GRACE QUALIFIES YOU FOR MINISTRY 123
- EMPOWERED BY GRACE 131
- LIVING BY GRACE 139
- YOUR KEY TO SUCCESS 149
- TRANSFORMED BY THE WORD 155
- WHY TESTS? 159
- FAITH IS THE BRIDGE 167
- HOW TO RELEASE FAITH 171
- WATER WALKERS 175
- THE SUPERNATURAL BECOMING NATURAL 185
- THE TRUE NATURE OF GOD 197
- SATAN, THE GREAT CON ARTIST 203
- SAVED LOST, SAVED LOST? 209

FOREWORD

I never knew being a Christian would be such hard work. I was told come receive Jesus and receive eternal life. So I did that, but now what! I thought it was a free gift, but living after the gift did not seem to work out very well. Was I really saved? If I was really saved, then why was life so frustrating? Did God really love me? Or did God only love me the moment I asked Jesus into my heart? I thought life would be full of the fruit I learned about in Sunday School: love, joy, peace, patience, kindness, goodness, faithfulness and self-control. But I can tell you after twenty years of being a Christian I really did not see much more fruit in my life than the day before I received this free gift named Jesus!

Do any of the above questions and situations resonate with you today? Does the Christian life just seem too hard? Does it seem like your life is a cycle of ups and downs and full of emotional turmoil never knowing how to make God pleased with you? Do you ever ask if Jesus really makes a difference for the "today" in your life? Or do you ever wonder if Jesus is only good for getting you to heaven?

I spent many years seeking to find out how to live the Christian life! I read every book I could read

FOREWORD

to gain knowledge from the so called "experts." I would look at myself and see my shortcomings and make a plan on how to improve and negate my shortcomings. If the plan did not work I would figure out how to tweak the plan. And every time it would seem that the plan would work for a while, but somewhere down the line it would come full circle back to where I started from in the beginning. "If I could just figure out the right plan."

I went to many conferences, seminars and even got my master's degree in Seminary. But no matter what pursuits I followed after the answers were never right! My Christian life was just not working! I could fake it with the best of them. I could compare myself to others and say that I was not doing too badly, but inside I could not lie to myself. I did not see any love, joy or peace in my life as a Christian.

So if any of the above describes you, or if you are curious to what the real Christian life is supposed to look like, then you have picked up the right book! I met Rick several years ago, and my life has never been the same! Rick has a way about him, and the way he has about him is because of Who he knows. You see Jesus came that we might have life and have it abundantly, and Rick has that life and he is ever-growing in more of the abundance of Jesus!

Jesus said that He came that we might experience a life full of joy and peace! In this book you will find out how to experience the "Jesus life" and why so many are not experiencing this life!

FOREWORD

In this book you will find the answers and keys to understanding what a life in Christ is all about! You will learn the importance of understanding your identity as God sees it! You will understand what the finished work of Jesus has to do with the Christian life. You will discover how your understanding that you live in the New Covenant impacts how you see your relationship with God and with others!

Most of all you will learn what grace has to do with life! Grace is a person and with that person you will experience real life! In this book, let Rick take you on a ride, experiencing grace as he experienced and continues to experience it in his life! It will be a fun ride and I can guarantee that as you read this book God will grant you the ability to receive and flow in His rhythms of Grace! Enjoy the ride and learn how to rest in Christ, so that life "makes sense" and exceeds far above and beyond what you could have ever imagined!

In Christ,

David Hawkins
Chaplain, Co-pastor Church In The Hamptons

> The only true righteousness of God cannot be achieved, it can only be received.

CHAPTER 1

REPENT!

Repent!!! What does the word repent really mean? I think most of us have been conditioned to believe that the word repent means to turn from sin. It may surprise many to know that repent does not actually mean to turn from sin but to change our mind or, more specifically, to change the way we are thinking or believing.

We can change our minds about anything, but Jesus called us to change our mind and believe the good news (Mk 1:15).

When Jesus preached and said, "Repent and believe the gospel," He was really telling us to change our mind by not trying to earn righteousness by works, but instead receive the only true acceptable righteousness that comes through faith. Under the New Covenant, righteousness is a free gift from God that can never be earned or achieved by any good work we do. The only true righteousness of God cannot be achieved, it can only be received. Right standing with God is a free gift from God through faith in Christ.

It's interesting to note that the Apostle John never once used the word repent in any of his writings. If repentance is so vital, then why didn't John use it? Instead, John used the word Believe. Believe the gospel. Believe in Jesus. However, we need to understand that to fully believe the good news and to receive the grace of God and the free gift of righteousness apart from works is to repent. Repentance means that you are no longer trying to pay for your own sins or trying to earn right standing with God. You recognize that Christ has already paid the price for all your sins and that you now freely receive forgiveness for all sins and right standing with God through faith in Christ.

John 1:12
> *"But as many as received him, to them gave he power to become the sons of God, even to them that believe on his name:"*

To repent means to turn from achieving to receiving and believing. To repent means that you fully believe what God has promised to do in the New Covenant.

Hebrews 10:17
> *"And their sins and iniquities will I remember no more."*

REPENT

What part of, "Our sins and iniquities He will remember no more," do we not understand?

When the Pharisees came to Jesus one day they asked Him, "What can we do to do the works of God?" Jesus told them, "This is the work of God that you believe in the One that He has sent." (Jn. 6:28-29).

Religion is all about doing something to become righteous before God but this is not how we receive true righteousness. True righteousness can never be achieved it can be only received as a gift. The Apostle Paul knew what it was like to try and earn his way with God under the law, but he had a divine revelation of the only true righteousness of God under the New Covenant

After Paul's revelation he says, "Now I just want to be found in Him, not having mine own righteousness, which is of the law, but that which is through the faith of Christ, the righteousness which is of God by faith." (Phil. 3:9).

Repentance means to firmly believe that God has forgiven us of all sin and has given us the free gift of righteousness apart from works

Some might ask, "So what are we really repenting from?" We are repenting from dead works! We are repenting from works that we often do to try and make ourselves right with God. We repent of all dead works of trying to earn God's approval or keep Gods approval. Today we are fully approved by God through Jesus plus nothing else. We repent from all dead works.

I'M SAVED! NOW WHAT?

Hebrews 6:1
> *"Therefore leaving the principles of the doctrine of Christ, let us go on unto perfection; not laying again the foundation of repentance from dead works, and of faith toward God."*

To continue in dead works is to stay stuck in religion and immaturity. Preachers who preach that the church needs to get busy doing stuff for God or God will turn His back on them, are really preaching a dead works theology that will keep the church bound in immaturity and carnality.

There is a big difference between dead works and good works. Good works are works that come as a result of right believing, because we believe that God unconditionally loves us and forgives us apart from our own works then this right believing moves us into doing good works. The works that I do are not because I'm afraid that God's going to disown me if I don't get busy and do a lot of stuff for Him. The good works are a result of believing God's great love for me. God is our Father not our Employer and we are His children not His employees.

Romans 4:5-9
> *"But to him who does not work but believes on Him who justifies the ungodly, his faith is accounted for righteousness."*

REPENT

To repent means that we refuse to work for righteousness.

God is the One Who has chosen to forgive us and to turn away from our sins. To repent means to believe that God has chosen to do this.

Those who do not embrace the New Covenant of God's grace and who refuse to believe that God completely forgives of all sin once and for all are really the ones who have not yet repented. They are un-repented

Those who believe that they will stand in judgment for sin have not yet repented, that is they still have not fully believed the good news of grace.

Grace preachers are often accused of promoting sin but who are the ones really promoting sin? Is it the grace preachers who preach that we are in right standing with God through faith or is it the preacher who continually preaches on sin every Sunday? If God remembers our sin no more then why are we still trying to remind people of their sins that God remembers no more? If the blood of Jesus was given to cleanse our conscience from all sin then why are we still promoting a sin conscience? Are we called to be preachers of sin or are we really called to be preachers of righteousness? The last time I looked we are suppose to preach the New Testament and righteousness that comes through faith in the finished work of the cross.

The ones promoting sin are the ones who are

always talking about it. Whatever we focus on is what will manifest in our lives. Many struggle with sin today because they are more focused on their sin then on Christ.

Sin is not the thing we are to be focused on. Jesus is the One we are to be looking to not sin. We are not changed by beholding sin but by beholding Jesus.

2 Corinthians 3:6
> *"Who also hath made us able ministers of the New Testament; not of the letter, but of the spirit: for the letter kills but the spirit giveth life."*

We need to understand that today we are under a New Covenant. We are no longer under the old but the new.

The old was about external demands but the new is about internal supply. Today we do not try and live by the demands of the letter; instead we live by the internal promptings of the Holy Spirit. One leads to life the other one leads to death.

Repent means that we no longer are to live by the law but by the Spirit of grace.

In fact the only way that we will ever produce vegetation for God is to be dead to the law.

Romans 7:4
> *"Wherefore, my brethren, ye also are*

> *become dead to the law by the body of Christ; that ye should be married to another, even to him who is raised from the dead, that we should bring forth fruit unto God."*

If we are to be dead to the law then why are so many still teaching the law as a way for Christians to conduct their lives? To mix law with grace is to teach another gospel.

We don't begin in the Spirit and then try and perfect ourselves by the flesh. We need to repent from trying to perfect ourselves by the flesh. We are only perfected by beholding and believing and the same way that we received Christ is the same way that we continue to walk in Him.

2 Corinthians 3:17-18
> *"But we all, with unveiled face, beholding as in a mirror the glory of the Lord, are being transformed into the same image from glory to glory, just as from the Lord, the Spirit."*

As we continue to behold what God has already done for us and in us then the Spirit of grace can then go to work to transform us into the image of Christ from glory to glory.

What are we to behold? Sin? No! We are to behold Christ and what He has already done in us

2 Corinthians 5:17
> *"Therefore if any man be in Christ, he is a new creature: old things are passed away; behold, all things are become new.... We are to always behold that all things have already been made new in Christ , no matter how we feel or how we fail we are not changed by beholding our feelings or failures but the truth that we are a new creation."*

We are not changed by beholding our sins, flaws and failures. We are only changed as we continue to behold who God says we are now in Christ (2 Cor. 5:17).

CHAPTER 2

BELIEVING THE RIGHT GOSPEL

The gospel is not the gospel of fear, condemnation and uncertainty but rather life, peace and joy in the Holy Ghost

If we believe the right gospel then there will be no fear of impending judgment or condemnation. If we believe the wrong gospel we might have short spurts of joy and peace but for the most part we will walk around with a lingering sense of condemnation and unworthiness. The Apostle John lists four critical things that every believer needs to understand, embrace and confess in order to stay free from the fear of judgment.

First, that God lives in us. Second, that we now live in God. Third, that God loves us unconditionally and completely. Fourth, as Jesus is so are we in this life.

If we do not believe that we are already complete in Christ and that God loves us unconditionally, chances are fear and condemnation rather than life and peace will dominate our life. If we have been convinced to believe that it's our performance and not the cross that justifies us before God, we will always walk with a lingering sense of uncertainty about judgment day. In the back of our minds we will wonder of we have really done enough to be pleasing to God

1 John 4:15-19 ESV
> *"Whoever confesses that Jesus is the Son of God, God abides in him, and he in God. So we have come to know and to believe the love that God has for us. God is love, and whoever abides in love abides in God, and God abides in him. By this is love perfected with us, so that we may have confidence for the day of judgment, because as he is so also are we in this world. There is no fear in love, but perfect love casts out fear. For fear has to do with punishment, and whoever fears has not been perfected in love. We love because he first loved us. ..."*

As we believe and receive Gods great love for us His perfect love for us will cast out all fear of judgment from our lives.

Those who fear judgment have not yet believed God's love for them. They still feel that God is not very happy with them and is going to punish them for not measuring up.

It is true that religion will drive you crazy. Religion has in fact has put many into the nut house. Many who are in mental institutions today are in there because in their own minds they feel they have committed the unpardonable sin. They have been convinced that God is going to punish and judge them for something that they have done and that there is no way for them to escape His eternal judgment.

What's even sadder is the fact that many Christians sit in church's today feeling the same way! Many Christians attend church every Sunday and hear the same condemning message that is filled with things like, "Jesus died for you! So what are you doing for Him?" "You will stand before God one day and He will show the 'This is your life video' and who knows you might even hear the words depart from me you didn't do enough to earn your right to come in."

Today, many Christians actually dread going to heaven for fear of the judgment day. But is this what the Bible really teaches? That we are supposed to fear judgment day? No, in fact it says the opposite! It says that if we are in Christ then we can look forward to the day of judgment. Why? Because as He is so are we in this world. If we have received Christ then we will stand before God on the judgment day in Christ and in Christ's righteousness not in our righteousness but in Christ's righteousness. This is what it means, as He is so are we in this world. We are righteous today not because of our righteousness but because we are now in the Righteous One, who is Christ. (2 Cor. 5:21)

The Bible says that perfect love casts out all fear of judgment but in most of our churches today fear seems to be the main way that we try to motivate Gods people into doing things.

We use fear to get them to serve, to give, to read their Bible and even attend church. Yes, there is a healthy fear of God that is a reverent respect for God and who God is, but fear of judgment is not a healthy fear and it is not the way to motivate any born again believer. God's people will be motivated by God's great love for them and the fact that He is for them and not against them, God's people will become highly motivated as they come into the truth that God has completely, once and for all time, forgiven them of all sin. As we preach the good news of God's love and grace the people of God will become highly motivated by the joy of knowing Him. You will not have to use fear or shame to try to motivate and prod them into doing things for God.

When people are in love and excited they will do much more than people who have been beaten and threatened.

Religion loves control. When leaders walk in religion they begin to think that it's their job to corral the sheep, police the sheep, beat the sheep and to make sure that the sheep are always behaving right. Through the years, religious leaders have set themselves up to actually become the way to know God. The church system has often become the only way that God's people can ever truly be fed or hear from God and, in extreme cases, the only way to even be forgiven and accepted by God. Now I know it is very important for the saints to assemble together and even the more as we see that day approaching, but when we imply that people cannot know God or be forgiven unless they are in the church building every Sunday then we have crossed the line.

I am a minister and presently pastor a church so I feel like I do have some authority to speak on this issue. Pastors and leaders are not called to police the sheep, corral the sheep or beat the sheep, we are called to feed the sheep and point them to their ultimate Shepherd who is Christ. Psalm 23 says that the Lord Is my Shepherd and in John 14:26 Jesus said the Holy Spirit Who He would send would be the One Who would ultimately teach us and lead each of us into all truth. 1 John 2:27 says we don't even need a man to teach us because the Holy Spirit would be our Teacher. Our way to God is not through a man or priest it is now through Jesus Christ that we have access to the Father.

Ephesians 2:18 KJV
"For through him we both have access by one Spirit unto the Father."

I'M SAVED! NOW WHAT?

Yes we respect leaders who the Lord has set in place to help us and teach us but we do not have to get to a leader in order to access God we have full access to God by the blood of the Lamb and by the Spirit of truth.

Our call as leaders is to feed the sheep with the gospel of grace that will then in turn free the sheep to enjoy a personal relationship with God.

Let me just say that I believe religion will be chopped in these last days! And God's people will be free to once again walk with God and know God in a very personal and intimate way. The axe is laid to the root of the religious tree and is being chopped!

In the early church, religion began its quest for control by following Paul around and preaching a mixed message of grace and law. They would say, "Yes, believe in Jesus for the initial salvation experience, but then after you are saved there are certain things that God requires you to do to maintain your righteousness." The message they preached was very deceptive because it made sense to the carnal mind and appealed to the flesh. It makes perfect sense that if we are saved we should then go out and and try doing our best to do righteous things for God. The problem with the mixed message was not that the doing of righteous things was bad but that the righteous things then turned into the way of our continued acceptance with God. As we believe in the finished work of the cross and receive God's unconditional love for us, righteous works will flow out from our lives and become the fruit of our right believing. But righteous works in themselves never justify us before God, only the blood does that.

Every letter that Paul wrote was aimed at bringing the church back to the finished work of Jesus. One by one, church by church, city by city believers were being seduced away from the cross and back into performance for righteousness.

One of the greatest needs in the church today is for leaders to trust that grace will work in God's people not only for salvation but for daily living. We must trust that God's grace is sufficient and allow grace to have space to work.

Many pastors are actually afraid of grace. Because they do not understand grace, they think too much grace is dangerous! That too much grace will cause the church to go wild in sin and reckless behavior. Many think that grace will only cause lazy couch potato type Christians, so pastors feel they are the ones who must keep the sheep in line, police the sheep, and drive the sheep into doing right things for God. Let me just say this, grace knows how to teach the sheep, lead the sheep and motivate the sheep far better than we could ever motivate them, but we must trust grace to work.

Titus 2:11-15
> *"For the grace of God that bringeth salvation hath appeared to all men, Teaching us that, denying ungodliness*

> *and worldly lusts, we should live soberly, righteously, and godly, in this present world; Looking for that blessed hope, and the glorious appearing of the great God and our Savior Jesus Christ; Who gave himself for us, that he might redeem us from all iniquity, and purify unto himself a peculiar people, zealous of good works. These things speak, and exhort, and rebuke with all authority. Let no man despise thee."*

What was the message to leaders here? That leaders were called to exhort God's people to learn to be led and taught by the Spirit of grace on how they should live and conduct their lives in this world. It did not say that leaders should tell people how to live but that leaders should exhort God's people to be taught by grace on how to live. Now we have a decision to make as leaders, are we going to trust grace to teach God's people how to live, are we going to trust grace to work in God's people or are we going to continue to try and do the job of grace?

If we will preach the gospel and continue to remind people of their new identity in Christ and trust grace to work we will see far different results than we have ever seen through religion.

The most dangerous leader is the one that has a great passion for people but does not believe in the power of grace to change people. Instead of trusting the Holy Spirit to change people they often resort to carnal methods to either try to change or contain people, because their containment methods seem to help prevent people from running wild in sin and they think they are successful in their methods. The question is in their hearts are they really free or just going through the motions?

God's plan is not for us to just go through the religious motions of Christian behavior but to be free and full of the life of Christ. For this to actually happen we must start believing the right gospel.

> As He is
> so are we
> in this
> world.

CHAPTER 3

NO MORE CONDEMNATION!

Someone had a dream about a woman who kept being punished for all the things that she did wrong. A certain man would follow her around wherever she went. Whenever she would make a mistake, he would immediately shake his head in disgust and then take off his belt and beat her. Even if she said one wrong word or even did the slightest wrong thing, the man would immediately punish her. Sometimes the punishment would go on for days. In the dream, the woman was seen limping around trying her best to put on a smile on her face and have a good attitude. No matter how hard she tried, she kept on doing things that would cause the man who followed her to punish her. It seemed like a hopeless situation for the woman, because no matter how hard she tried she couldn't do enough good to keep from being punished.

Now the woman in the dream really represents

much of the church, who often feels like they must somehow earn God's favor through their own perfect behavior and performance. The man beating the woman does not represent God, but really represents their own heart that continually condemns them and punishes them for even the slightest mistake.

Because most Christians do not understand God's grace (undeserved, unearned favor of God), they are continually trying to please God through their own good behavior, works, and performance. And of course when they do not feel like they are performing well or measuring up, then the man (their own heart) punishes them.

Religion loves control. Many religious leaders really love for people to be kept needy, immature, and defeated because it keeps people co-dependent on them and on a religious system. It also keeps people bound to a religious system that only provides temporary relief or victory, but keeps them mostly in a place of false guilt, condemnation, and defeat. One major reason that the Pharisees hated Jesus was because He was setting people free from condemnation and defeat and bringing them into His kingdom of love, joy, and peace. When the Pharisees saw Jesus doing this, then they knew that they were losing control of the people to Jesus. It's time for God's people to be set free from religion to follow Jesus.

The only way that the church will ever be free from her own vicious cycle of failings and beatings is through a revelation of God's grace. God's grace is the unearned, undeserved favor of God. God's grace is given to us as a gift from God, and not of works. Those in grace do not strive for perfection; they instead rest in the perfection of Christ. Those in grace do not live for Jesus; they live from Jesus because they understand that they are in Christ and Christ is now living in them (Galatians 2:20). Grace also delivers us from all self beatings and condemnation so that we can experience the continual peace of God.

The kingdom of God is not condemnation but love, peace, and joy in the Holy Ghost. God does not want us to spend our entire Christian lives in condemnation and defeat but in love, peace, and joy. Condemnation does not expand God's kingdom. The fruit of the Spirit being manifest in and through our lives is what expands the kingdom of God. Grace does not require our perfect behavior; it only requires our simple trust and faith in the finished work of the cross.

When the New Covenant speaks about obedience, it is mostly speaking about obedience to the faith. We are saved by grace through faith. Grace delivers us from our own fruitless fleshly attempts of trying our best to live for God, and instead surrender to the One Who now is at work in us. As our heart is established in grace, then it no longer tries to earn God's acceptance through performance. Neither does it try to keep the law for righteousness. Those in grace understand that righteousness is a gift to us because of Christ's obedience. As we walk in grace we will finally be able to get away from the beatings brought on to us because of the flesh and the law.

It's amazing how Romans chapter 8 begins:

"There is therefore now no condemnation for those who are in Christ Jesus, who walk not after the flesh but after the Spirit."

The word "no" here means never. Never is there any more condemnation for those who are in Christ. God did not send His Son to condemn us but to save us and to set us free from all condemnation.

Those walking in grace do not focus on their failures, but their focus is kept on Christ, Who is the Author and Finisher of our faith and it's kept on God's unconditional love for them.

God in His mercy sent us help; His name is Jesus. God sent Jesus to deliver us from ourselves and our powerless attempts to fulfill His law. Jesus took the punishment for the law that we could not keep so that we wouldn't have to die, and could go free and have eternal life. Jesus gave us the gift of righteousness so that we could be righteous and holy before God and meet all the requirements of the law. We have peace with God through what Jesus did for us in His death, burial, and resurrection. And we have favor with God that is unearned and undeserved favor. That's grace.

Believing this, your heart must be settled

without a doubt, knowing that Jesus did this because He loves you and wants to make your heart sound, secure, stable, and firm. God wants our hearts to be established in His grace to keep us from condemnation and self beatings. God's will is to never shrink back from Him, but for us to always confidently draw near to Him. Any time we feel unworthy and condemned, this is not coming from God... it is either coming from the devil, who is the accuser, or from our own hearts.

Romans 8:1
> *"There is therefore now no condemnation to them which are in Christ Jesus, who walk not after the flesh, but after the Spirit."*

Romans 5:17
> *"For if by one man's offense death reigned by one; much more they which receive abundance of grace and of the gift of righteousness shall reign in life by one, Jesus Christ."*

Titus 3:5
> *"Not by works of righteousness which we have done, but according to his mercy he saved us, by the washing of regeneration, and renewing of the Holy Ghost."*

I'M SAVED! NOW WHAT?

Romans 11:6
> *"And if by grace, then is it no more of works: otherwise grace is no more grace. But if it be of works, then it is no more grace: otherwise work is no more work."*

CHAPTER 4

SELF RIGHTEOUSNESS OR FAITH RIGHTEOUSNESS?

Is Jesus coming back just to judge us for all our doing? And if so, how much doing will be enough to be acceptable to Him? Does anyone really know? Do those who teach and preach that we should get busy doing things for God really know how much doing is enough? Is salvation really based on what we do for Christ or what Christ has already done for us and what He is now presently doing in us? Which message produces the most peace? The one that says get busy doing stuff for God or God may not be pleased with you? Or is it the message of the cross that says it has already been done? Jesus paid the price. It finished!

We often preach a message that is full of double talk and brings confusion to those who hear it. A mixed message will produce a mixed up people.

For example, we say come to Jesus without works, without one plea, it's grace, undeserved, unearned favor from God and then when someone receives Christ we almost immediately bring out the to-do-list of things that they must follow. Then they begin "doing" in order to maintain their rightness with God. What happened to the "it's a free gift" thing?

If it's by our works that we are saved and not just the cross, then why don't we just tell people from the beginning that salvation is really not free, that there are strings attached? That God in the end is really going to judge you more on things you do for Him like Bible reading, church attendance, tithing, prayer and works. The cross was just the hook to get you in but your own works are really what keeps you in.

I recently watch a Christian motivational program on TV that said, "It's not just about believing, it's really about your doing. Are you doing enough for Jesus? Are you a fan or a follower? Jesus died for you so what are you now doing for Him?" In a flash they then said, "It's really not just about your doing, it's about your believing in Him but believing isn't enough because it's really about your doing and really doing isn't enough either, if what your doing isn't being done with love for God. So are you believing enough? Are you doing enough? Are you loving God enough? Do you love God with all your

SELF RIGHTEOUSNESS OR FAITH RIGHTEOUSNESS?

heart, mind, soul and strength? Are you really a follower of Jesus or just a fan? Are you really doing enough? Maybe you need to get busy doing more? Are you kind enough? Are you loving enough? Are you reading your Bible enough? Are you praying enough, are you giving enough?"

So after watching this program for 30 minutes my only thought was, "Enough is enough!" It's time for Christians to stop the insane double talk and get off the religious tread mill of, "Am I doing enough?" And instead learn to simply rest in Christ and believe what He did at the cross was enough! When Jesus said it is finished, He was saying all that needed to be done was done through My death. Now He calls us to cease from all our doing for righteousness and enter into His rest (Hebrews 4:10). Jesus has called us to believe and receive all that He has already done and given to us makes us complete in Him and then simply to rely and respond to what He is now prompting to do in and through us.

What am I called to do? I'm called to do whatever He shows me to do. Isn't that how Jesus did it? He did the things the Father showed Him to do. Jesus was led by the Spirit, Who lived in Him. We are called to now live the same way. It's not about us getting a list out and then trying to do everything on the list. This will either drive you crazy or make you hypocritical. No, it's about walking in peace with God and whatever He prompts you to do then you do what He shows you to do.

I'M SAVED! NOW WHAT?

The Bible is not a to-do-manual, it's about Emmanuel. It's about God with us and now God living in us and through us. This new living way, that God has called us to walk in, is called newness of life or walking after the Spirit and not after the letter. The letter kills but the Spirit gives life.

Those who are involved in a letter, performance driven to-do gospel, for the most part lack joy and reek with criticism and judgment and to be honest they make a very poor witness for Christ. Self righteous dead works do not glorify God, they only glorify the flesh. Dead works will make you critical towards others. Much of the world does not want the Christian way because they often see people in church who are more critical, judgmental and more depressed than those who do not even know Christ. Condemnation is not a great way to attract people to Christ but when the world begins to see a church filled with life, joy and peace then they will want what we have. For the church to begin to express the true kingdom of God they must turn from self righteousness and dead works and turn back to faith righteousness.

Self righteousness is always concerned with what it is doing to become or maintain its righteousness. Self righteousness will always make you conscience of self but faith righteousness will make you conscience of Christ. When we are conscience of Christ, then perfect peace will come whose mind is stayed on Him.

SELF RIGHTEOUSNESS OR FAITH RIGHTEOUSNESS?

Faith righteousness is a free gift given to us by God, apart from works (Romans 5). Because of Christ's obedience, we are made righteous, period (2 Corinthians 5:21). And we are never to put a question mark where God puts a period.

Once you have received the free gift of righteousness you are righteous and nothing can ever undo what God has made you to be. Sin can unravel your life but not your righteous nature in Christ. Once you are born again, God did something extra ordinary! He joined Himself with you and now nothing will ever be able to separate you from Him again. You are stuck with God forever! (Romans 8:31-39)

1 Corinthians 6:17

> *"But he that is joined unto the Lord is one spirit."*

As you see yourself one with the Lord, every definition of separation or distance from God is cancelled. Now you don't see God way up in heaven and out of our reach but now you see that God is in us and even one with us. Like the Apostle Paul says in His famous sermon on Mars Hill.

Acts 17:28

> *"For in him we live, and move, and have our being; as certain also of your own poets have said, For we are also his offspring."*

I'M SAVED! NOW WHAT?

Romans 5:19 says that we are not made righteous because of our obedience but Christ's obedience. As we believe this truth it will disarm the devil, the accuser, in our lives. The devil cannot accuse someone who fully believes who God says that they are now in Christ apart from their performance.

This is why the Scripture says that the devil was disarmed when Jesus nailed the law, which was based on our performance, to the cross (Col 2:14-15). If the devil comes to me and says, "You're not doing enough," I simply tell slew foot, "It's not my doing that makes me righteous but what Christ has already done that makes righteous!" Many leaders in church today actually re-arm the devil by turning God's people back to a law based, performance gospel. The devil is having a hay day with many Christians who do not understand who they are now in Christ. If you are in Christ, then as He is so are you! Is Jesus Righteous? Then so are you, for as He is so are you in this life. (I John 4:17)

Much of our so-called spiritual warfare has been created by our own wrong believing. As we begin to believe right and submit to the truth of the gospel, then we will see the devil has already been defeated and that he is more terrified of us then we should ever be of him. (James 4:7)

So what about 1 Peter 5:8?

"Be sober, be vigilant; because your adversary the devil, as a roaring lion,

SELF RIGHTEOUSNESS OR FAITH RIGHTEOUSNESS?

> *walks about, seeking whom he may devour:"*

The ones that Satan is seeking to devour are those who are in religious deception and still believe in a performance driven gospel for righteousness.

Romans 10:3-4
> *"For they being ignorant of God's righteousness, and going about to establish their own righteousness, have not submitted themselves unto the righteousness of God. For Christ is the end of the law for righteousness to everyone who believes."*

To disarm the devil we must submit only to the righteousness of God which is by faith in Christ. To re-arm the devil is to turn back to self righteousness. As we submit to God and resist the devil then he will flee from us (James 4:7). The devil does not want to even be near to the Christian that has awakened to faith righteousness and grace.

Self righteousness always has self in mind for righteousness or, "Am I doing enough to be right with God?" This is self righteousness. Faith righteousness always has Christ in mind and the cross in mind. Faith righteousness agrees with the cross and says, "Yes, Christ did all that so that I might become the righteousness of God in Him and now I receive freely the abundance of God's grace and the free gift of righteousness." (2 Corinthians 5:17). It is only as we choose to receive the abundance of God's grace and the free gift of righteousness that we will ever be victorious in this life!

As we renew our minds to the truth of faith righteousness, this truth will enable us to reign in this life by One, Jesus Christ.

Self righteousness will always keep our attention set on self or, "Am I doing enough to please God?" Any message that moves our attention away from the finished work of Christ for righteousness and back to self is not the gospel of Christ. Our attention is not to be on self but on Christ. Perfect peace only comes to those whose minds are stayed on Him. We are also encouraged to set our affections on things above where Christ sits. There is a big reason for this because the Bible says that right now we are also seated with Him. In God's eyes we are not still trying through our own works to get into Gods kingdom. In God's eyes we are already there in Christ!

Ephesians 2:5-6
> *"Even when we were dead in sins, hath quickened us together with Christ, (by grace ye are saved;) And hath raised us up together, and made us sit together in heavenly places in Christ Jesus:"*

Why did God do all this for us? There is only one answer and that's love.

SELF RIGHTEOUSNESS OR FAITH RIGHTEOUSNESS?

Ephesians 2:4
> *"But God, who is rich in mercy, for his great love wherewith he loved us."*

Faith does not see itself trying to get into God's kingdom. Faith sees that we are already in God's kingdom because of what Jesus has already accomplished for us (Col 1:13). Yes, there is a future manifestation of what we are already a part of, but we need to see that in Christ we are already citizens of the kingdom of God and God is not going to revoke our passport if He doesn't see enough works accomplished in our work book.

When we stand before God, He will see us one of two ways. He will either see us in Christ or in Adam. When you received Christ you were removed from Adam and placed into Christ.

Now that we are in Christ, we are no longer in Adam. We are now in the Righteous One, who is Christ. We need to not only believe in Christ but we need to believe into Christ. Many believe in Christ but not into Christ. Until we believe into Christ we will always see ourselves somewhat incomplete. To believe into Christ means more than just believing what He has done for me. It is believing what Christ has done with the old me and what He has now done in me.

Jesus did much more than just forgive our sins, He made us into a new creation in Him. We were actually baptized into Christ and made to be one with Him.

2 Corinthians 5:17
> *"Therefore if any man be in Christ, he is a new creature: old things are passed away; behold, all things are become new."*

The old thing that passed away was my old nature that once lived in Adam. That old man was crucified with Christ and the new me is now one with Christ. I am in Him and He is in me. It is by faith that we come to fully understand this. I am now a new creation in Christ, old is gone the new has come. Again never put a question mark where God has put a period.

Romans 6:4
> *"Therefore we are buried with him by baptism into death: that like as Christ was raised up from the dead by the glory of the Father, even so we also should walk in newness of life."*

We are not half old and half new. We are a new creation in Christ. Yes, we still have the same old body that most of us would love to trade in right now for a new one. We still have some old mind sets that need to catch up with our new created self. But as we believe and confess the truth about who God's says we are now in Christ, we will then begin to see transformation take place from the inside out.

Not only have we believed a mixed gospel, we

SELF RIGHTEOUSNESS OR FAITH RIGHTEOUSNESS?

have also believed in a mixed nature. We have been taught that we have two natures in us, that we possess the old nature and the new nature in the same house. This is not true. Today we have one new created nature created in Christ and the old is dead and gone! When Jesus came in, He did not ask the old nature to move over and make room for Him. Jesus is not roommates with the devil. Jesus evicted the old man!

The mind that is set on self righteousness will always keep people away from grace and keep Christ from working in their lives but as we embrace grace and faith righteousness His resurrection power that is in us will quicken our mortal bodies. (Romans 8) Either we (flesh) are working or grace is working but both cannot work at the same time. We must give up our futile efforts of trying to change by our own human effort and instead trust grace.

To know that we have received the free gift of righteousness and that we are a new creation in Christ is the key which will set us free from the dominion of sin and allow grace to work in our lives. Grace can only reign through faith righteousness. (Romans 5:21)

"Well what if I sin? What happens then? Do I then have to be born again all over again?" In short, no!

Let me ask you a question "If you fall into water you may get wet but you will not turn into a fish will you? Yes, there are earthly consequences to falling in sin but your falling into sin will not change your righteous nature.

To illustrate this, I had a friend once who was talking on his phone and because he wasn't paying attention he fell right into his pool fully clothed while on his phone! He didn't turn into a fish but he did suffer the consequences. He was soaking wet and his phone ruined. His communication was also affected for a moment but he did not turn into a fish.

Sin can unravel your life, sin will burn you, sin will hurt you that's why God says don't do it! But sin will not cause you to be unborn. The prodigal son suffered the consequences of sin but he never stopped being the father's son.

There are only two kinds of people on earth those in Adam and those in Christ. There is no middle man. You're either in Adam or in Christ.

I Corinthians 15:22, 45 and 47 in Adam all died but in Christ all are made alive. The first Adam was made a living soul but the last Adam was made a life giving Spirit! Today you are either dead or alive. You are either dead in Adam or alive in Christ. The good news is that you can easily be made to be one alive in Christ simply by choosing to believe and receive what Christ has already done for us.

2 Corinthians 5:21
> *"For he hath made him to be sin for us, who knew no sin; that we might be made the righteousness of God in him."*

SELF RIGHTEOUSNESS OR FAITH RIGHTEOUSNESS?

The mindset of self righteousness will keep you away from what grace has already made available to you. Self righteousness puts more faith in what it does for Christ, more than in what Christ has already done for it.

Why can't people just accept that they are righteous by faith in what Christ has done? It's called the flesh loves glory. Flesh wants to take credit for its right standing with God but we must put our foot down and say no to flesh that wants to take credit for what Christ has already accomplished. This is what it means to deny your flesh. We are to deny flesh from taking credit for what Christ has already accomplished. (Romans 4:3-5)

We must refuse to earn or work for righteousness. Righteousness is a free gift not something earned. Period. As I believe this the Bible says I will experience His life and peace (Romans 5:1). If I choose not to believe this I will walk in condemnation.

Romans 4:5-8

But to him that works not, but believes on him that justifies the ungodly, his faith is counted for righteousness.] Even as David also described the blessedness of the man, unto whom God imputes righteousness without works, Saying , Blessed (Happy to the point where others will be envious) are they (who know their) iniquities are forgiven, and whose (who know and believe that their) sins are covered. Blessed is the man to whom the Lord will not impute sin.

Romans five speaks of this free gift of righteousness given to us because of Christ's obedience. If we will believe that we are righteous because of Christ's obedience then grace is able to go to work in us to change us and free us. Grace is not a doctrine, grace is the Spirit of Christ that now works in us and grace can only work through faith righteousness.

We who believe are now in Christ and not in Adam. The old is gone the new has come.

Galatians 6:15
"For in Christ Jesus neither circumcision avails anything, nor uncircumcision, but a new creature."

In Christ it's about a new creation. It's not about what you do. It is about what has been done and what God in Christ has made you to be. In Christ, we are now a new creation that has never existed. We are not re-created after the first Adam but after the last Adam, Who is Christ.

We must see ourselves now fully in Christ not in Adam and not in both. We are not in both Adam and Christ it's one or the other. If you are in Christ

SELF RIGHTEOUSNESS OR FAITH RIGHTEOUSNESS?

then you are a new creation in Christ. This is key to your transformation.

Once we are convinced of our permanent position now in Christ and that our righteousness is a free gift because of Christ's obedience, grace will begin to flow in and through our lives.

2 Peter 1: 4-9 gives us a major key to partaking of His divine nature, deliverance, freedom and fruitfulness. It is to firmly know and believe that we have been, once and for all time, fully forgiven and purged from all sin. Not some sin but all sin. God no longer wants us to have a sin conscience but a righteous conscience. A righteous conscience will cause us to partake of His divine nature. A sin conscience will keep us from partaking of His divine nature. We are not doing the church a favor by constantly wagging our boney fingers at them and pointing out sin. God has called us to be preachers of the New Testament not the old. Under the old there was constant reminding of sin but in the New Testament God says, "I will forgive and remember their sins no more." Today we are called to remind people about God's crazy love for them and about who they now are in Christ. As God's people embrace His precious promises for them they will begin to partake of the diving nature that has been created in them and escape the corruption that's in the world because of lust

I'M SAVED! NOW WHAT?

2 Peter 1:4

> *"Whereby are given unto us exceeding great and precious promises: that by these ye might be partakers of the divine nature, having escaped the corruption that is in the world through lust."*

CHAPTER 5

AWAKE TO RIGHTEOUSNESS

Faith righteousness is crucial to seeing everything else work in our lives. Faith righteousness is the only true righteousness that is acceptable with God. There are only two kinds of righteousness faith or self righteousness. God's word tells us to seek first the kingdom of God and His righteousness and all other things will be added to us.

In Romans 10 we see the Apostle Paul praying for his fellow kinsmen:

Romans 10:1-4
> "Brethren, my heart's desire and prayer for Israel is that they might be saved. For I bear them record that they have a zeal for God but not according to knowledge. For they being ignorant of Gods righteousness and going about to

establish their own righteousness have not submitted to the righteousness of God, for Chris is the end of the law for righteousness to everyone who believes."

Self righteousness comes to an end and true righteousness of God begins when we quit trying to establish our own righteousness through our own good works and simply believe that Christ's obedience to the cross was sufficient to make us 100% righteous before God. "How do I know when I'm engaged in self righteousness?"

Self righteousness is based on our own conduct, our own works, our own performance and self effort. If we feel like we are not measuring up and that somehow we need to do more to become more right with God then it is self righteousness. If we are feeling that God is not very pleased with me because I have not behaved like I should then that's a self righteousness attitude. Faith righteousness believes its righteousness is based solely on Jesus Christ and the finished work of the cross and is a result of the new birth.

Faith righteousness is not about us and what we do for Jesus, it's really all about what Jesus has already done for us. The righteousness of God is a done deal and can only be received as a gift by faith and never achieved by any work we do.

In faith righteousness I'm not trying to get more righteous, holy, or redeemed. I agree with God's word that I am already righteous, holy and redeemed in Christ. When I first received Jesus, a supernatural thing took place called the new birth. When the new birth took place the Bible says that our old sin nature was taken away and put to death! And God put a new nature in its place. Our new nature has now been joined with the Lord Himself so as He is so are we in this life. (1 John 4:17) So today we are as righteous right now as Jesus is. Faith righteousness believes this; we have been made the righteousness of God in Christ. (2 Corinthians 5:21)

Self righteousness does not believe this. Self righteousness believes we are initially saved by grace but we must maintain our right standing with God through works. When we turn from grace and faith righteousness back to the law for righteousness we have fallen from grace! Many in the church today have fallen away from grace and back to the law of self effort.

Now, before we go on, let's look at just a few Scriptures of many that confirm our new righteous nature in Christ.

2 Corinthians 5:17 AMP

> *"Therefore if any person is ingrafted in Christ (the Messiah) he is a new creation (a new creature altogether); the old previous moral and spiritual condition has passed away, behold the fresh and new has come!"*

2 Corinthians 5:21
> *"For he hath made him to be sin for us, who knew no sin; that we might be made the righteousness of God in him."*

1 Corinthians 1:30
> *"But of him are you in Christ Jesus, who of God is made unto us wisdom, and righteousness, and sanctification, and redemption"*

These Scriptures confirm that when we were born again, we were also made to be everything that Jesus is right now! This was not by our doing, but was all God's doing! When we first received Jesus, God took away the old, re-created us and put us into Christ and now all things have been made new and are of God. All means ALL. In your new born again spirit, all things are new and of God

Righteousness is what we have been given and righteousness is what we have now been made to be in Christ.

It's is vital for us to know this and believe this because it is only through faith righteousness, believing we are fully righteous in Christ, that grace is then enabled to work in our lives! And it is only through faith righteousness that we can enter the rest of God and partake of all that we have already been given in Christ.

Have you ever taken a water hose that was

fully turned on and then pinched it off? When you pinch the water hose off the water flow stops. This is in essence what happens when you turn from believing that you are already righteous in Christ and turn back to self righteousness.

Self righteousness restricts the flow of God's grace in your life but faith righteousness releases God's grace to flow. I am seeing that faith righteousness is the key to everything that God has already given us. It is through faith righteousness that we will either walk in victory or live in defeat in this life.

When the Apostle Paul speaks of fighting the fight of faith, he was really talking about holding on to faith righteousness! He was telling us that there are a lot of elements in this world that are constantly trying to move us away from faith righteousness and back into a self righteousness based on works and the law of self effort. Sad to say, one of our greatest contenders has always been legalistic religion.

I have always said the place that you need to make sure that you have the full armor of God on is in most churches. Because many are ignorant of faith righteousness often times the message you will here will be more about you doing things to either get right with God or stay right with God. It is seldom about what Christ has already done and more about what you need to do.

How do we recognize when we are hearing a message that may sound good but is laced with self righteousness? When a message is always referring to what you need to do in order to be acceptable and pleasing to God then it is a self righteous message. Likewise when a message that will often imply that what you're doing is still not enough to be pleasing to God, it is self righteous. When you hear messages like, "Jesus died for you so what are you doing for Him?" This may sound right and even get a lot of amens, but this kind of message is simply an attempt to motivate you into doing through guilt and shame.

Guilt, shame, and condemnation are never the way that God motivates His people. The Bible is clear that love is to be the only motivation behind all we do. If what we do is not motivated by love, then all we are doing really profits nothing.

1 Corinthians 13:3
> *"And though I bestow all my goods to feed the poor, and though I give my body to be burned, and have not love, it profits me nothing."*

Love is to be our great motivator. The only way we can ever love is to first believe and receive the great unconditional love that God has for us. True love always begins with God's love for us, not our love for God.

1 John 4:10

> "In this is love: not that we loved God, but that He loved us and sent His Son to be the propitiation (the atoning sacrifice) for our sins."

1 John 4:9

> "In this the love of God was made manifest (displayed) where we are concerned: in that God sent His Son, the only begotten or unique Son, into the world so that we might live through Him."

God's great motivation for all He has done, and is now doing in us, is love. John 3:16 teaches for God so loved us that He gave His only begotten son to not only die for us but so that we could also be righteous and complete and even live our new lives through Him. One huge thing that we have not understood is that Jesus did not come just to die for our sins but He came to give us a new righteous nature and a new way to live.

The Apostle Paul had an incredible revelation about this new way of living in Christ that took place through the new birth. We, like Paul, also need to fully understand what Jesus came to do.

Galatians 2:19-21 MSG

> "What actually took place is this: I tried

keeping rules and working my head off to please God, and it didn't work. So I quit being a "law man" so that I could be God's man. Christ's life showed me how, and enabled me to do it. I identified myself completely with him. Indeed, I have been crucified with Christ. My ego is no longer central. It is no longer important that I appear righteous before you or have your good opinion, and I am no longer driven to impress God. Christ lives in me. The life you see me living is not "mine," but it is lived by faith in the Son of God, who loved me and gave himself for me. I am not going to go back on that. Is it not clear to you that to go back to that old rule-keeping, peer-pleasing religion would be an abandonment of everything personal and free in my relationship with God? I refuse to do that, to repudiate God's grace. If a living relationship with God could come by rule-keeping, then Christ died unnecessarily."

The old was about rule keeping for righteousness but the new way is about all about being righteous in Christ. It's all about Christ being in me and Christ living in me and though me! It's about being filled with the life of Christ.. Jesus didn't say that I came to give you a new set of rules but I have come that you might have life and have life more abundantly.

John 10:10
> "The thief cometh not, but for to steal, and to kill, and to destroy: I am come that they might have life, and that they might have it more abundantly."

The biggest way that the thief, who is the devil, steals what God has already freely given to us in Christ is to turn us away from grace and faith righteousness back to a system of performance and rule keeping for righteousness but Paul said to go back to the old rule keeping system is to abandoned all that Christ came to do.

Hebrews 10:8-10 ESV
> "When he said above, 'You have neither desired nor taken pleasure in sacrifices and offerings and burnt offerings and sin offerings' (these are offered according to the law), then he added, 'Behold, I have come to do your will.' He does away with the first in order to establish the second. And by that will we have been sanctified through the offering of the body of Jesus Christ once for all."

God never did take pleasure in the old law, rule keeping, and sacrificial way of doing things because it could never make anyone righteous before Him. But where the old way failed, Christ came and accomplished and He did it once and for all time!

Romans 5:17-21
> "For if by one man's offence death reigned by one; much more they which receive abundance of grace and of the gift of righteousness shall reign in life by one, Jesus Christ.) Therefore as by the offence of one judgment came upon all men to condemnation; even so by the righteousness of one the free gift came upon all men unto justification of life. For as by one man's disobedience many were made sinners, so by the obedience of one shall many be made righteous."

I hate to pop your bubble, but it is not because of our great obedience that we have been made righteous before God. It's through the obedience of Christ that we are now righteous. Righteousness always begins and ends with Jesus, not you. Any message that you hear that even implies that your right standing with God has to do with you is not the gospel of Christ. The gospel of you is not the gospel of Christ!

We are saved, redeemed, holy and sanctified because of one man's obedience and that one man is Jesus, not you. And it begins and ends with Him not you.

If we turn from Christ for righteousness and back to ourselves, we will only experience great disappointment, frustration and condemnation. Condemnation, frustration, fear, shame and feelings of unworthiness are all the result of believing in the gospel of you.

Today we are righteous and holy because we are in Him Who is righteous and holy, so as He is so are we in his life. (1 John 4:17)

2 Corinthians 5:17
> *"Therefore if any man be in Christ, he is a new creature: old things are passed away; behold, all things are become new."*

2 Corinthians 5:21
> *"For he hath made him to be sin for us, who knew no sin; that we might be made the righteousness of God in him."*

2 Corinthians 11:2-4
> *"For I am jealous over you with godly jealousy: for I have espoused you to one husband, that I may present you as a chaste virgin to Christ. But I fear, lest by any means, as the serpent beguiled Eve*

> *through his subtlety, so your minds should be corrupted from the simplicity that is in Christ."*

It does not matter what your past is. Once you receive Christ you are as a chaste Virgin. Before Him you are as pure as the driven snow! You are as pure and innocent as a chaste virgin. This is how God sees you in Christ and this is how God wants you to now see yourself.

We are not to allow the devil to move us away from the simplicity that is in Christ. This simplicity says I am who God says I now am in Christ. Period!

Galatians 6:15
> *"For neither is circumcision now of any importance, nor uncircumcision, but only a new creation the result of a new birth and a new nature in Christ Jesus, the Messiah."*

God is telling us that it's not about what you do or don't do, it's about what's Christ has already accomplished. It's about the new creation. The new you that's now in Christ...this is your new identity (2 Corinthians 5:17). God wants us to see who we are now in Christ and as we see our new self then all else will flow out from this.

Colossians 1:25-28

> *"Whereof I am made a minister, according to the dispensation of God which is given to me for you, to fulfill the word of God; Even the mystery which hath been hid from ages and from generations, but now is made manifest to his saints: To whom God would make known what is the riches of the glory of this mystery among the Gentiles; which is Christ in you, the hope of glory: Whom we preach, warning every man, and teaching every man in all wisdom; that we may present every man perfect in Christ Jesus:"*

Our main call is to teach Christ is in you, the hope of glory and to present every man already perfect in Christ.

We have seen the bumper stickers that say, "I'm not perfect just forgiven?" Well in Christ you are not just forgiven you are perfect

In Christ we are forgiven, chaste and perfect. We are already complete in Him. You are heaven ready, but now to become earth ready we need to believe what God's word says about our new true spiritual condition. We are as righteous as we are ever going to be.

If we are born again and in Christ then we are never to question what God has already accomplished for us in Christ. I am righteous. I am holy. I am all these things because I'm in Christ. What God has made me to be does not fluctuate. My righteousness in Christ does not fluctuate with my behavior, or how I feel. Your righteousness or right standing with God is because of Jesus plus nothing else. It is not Jesus plus what I do. It's Jesus plus nothing else.

Once you settle this truth about faith righteousness in your heart and you believe the truth about righteousness of God by faith then you can move out of condemnation and out of full time ministry to yourself. You can then move into the full time ministry that God has called and prepared for you to walk in even before the foundation of the world..

Self is not my source for righteousness; Jesus is my only source for all true acceptable righteousness with God. (2 Corinthians 5:21)

Today a lot of people in church have walked in a lot of self righteousness, but the good news is that many are waking up to the only true approved righteousness of God that comes through faith in Christ alone. And because they are waking up to faith righteousness they are being delivered from the dominion of sin.

2 Peter 1:3-4

"According as his divine power hath given unto us all things that pertain unto life and godliness, through the knowledge

> *of him that hath called us to glory and virtue: Whereby are given unto us exceeding great and precious promises: that by these ye might be partakers of the divine nature, having escaped the corruption that is in the world through lust."*

2 Peter 1:4-9

> *"He that lacks these things is blind, and cannot see afar off, and has forgotten that he was purged from his old sins."*

What things was Paul speaking about? Paul was speaking about righteous works and fruit. Religion will tell you that if you lack fruit it's because you're not trying hard enough to produce the fruit. Paul said that because we have forgotten that we have been purged from our old sins which include all sins and even the sin nature.

Fruit comes as a result of our believing that we are 100% forgiven and new in Christ. Right believing will lead to right living. We are transformed from the inside out, not the outside in.

2 Corinthians 3:9

> *"For if the ministration of condemnation be glory, much more doth the ministration of righteousness exceed in glory."*

I'M SAVED! NOW WHAT?

The ministration of righteousness will always exceed in glory. As we understand that we are the righteousness of God in Christ we will begin to experience His exceeding glory.

God's ultimate purpose is to manifest His exceeding glory in us and through us! There is only one way that this is going to happen, it will only happen through the ministration of righteousness that comes through faith.

When Moses came down with the law there was glory on Moses' face. Even with the law, which was called the ministry of death and condemnation, there was a certain amount of glory. Under the New Covenant of grace and faith righteousness there will be a manifestation of great exceeding glory. This exceeding glory in the last days will be the visible glory of God that will be seen on all those who believe that Christ is the end of the law for righteousness.

Isaiah 60:1-3
> *"Arise, shine, for your light has come, and the glory of the LORD has risen upon you. For behold, darkness shall cover the earth, and thick darkness the peoples; but the LORD will arise upon you, and his glory will be seen upon you. And nations shall come to your light, and kings to the brightness of your rising."*

In the last days, which by the way I do believe

that we are living in right now, there will be gross darkness and great glory at the same time. I heard Bob Jones say once, "In the last days we will see both gory and glory simultaneously."

This is the worlds' darkest time and the church's brightest time. It's time for the church to shine! And she will shine as she moves away from self righteousness and wakes up once again to God's righteousness which can only be realized through faith in Christ.

God's exceeding glory is made manifest only through the ministration of His righteousness according to the New Covenant of grace.

As we seek first the kingdom of God and His righteousness then all these other things will be added to us. If we will simply put these two things first everything else will work and flow including grace. Grace only works through faith righteousness. Grace cannot work in self righteousness.

Grace only works through faith righteousness, which will result in freedom, joy and life.

Romans 5:20-21

> "But then Law came in, [only] to expand and increase the trespass [making it more apparent and exciting opposition]. But where sin increased and abounded, grace (God's unmerited favor) has surpassed it and increased the more and super-abounded. So that, [just] as sin has

> *reigned in death, [so] grace (His unearned and undeserved favor) might reign also through righteousness (right standing with God) which issues in eternal life through Jesus Christ (the Messiah, the Anointed One) our Lord."*

The law (self righteousness) only gives strength to sin and its result is always frustration, condemnation and death. In faith righteousness grace is enabled to work to bring forth life.

Someone once said, "There is only about 12 inches between heaven and hell." That's the distance between what is already a reality in your heart and what you believe in your mind. What we believe will cause us to live a defeated Christian life or a victorious one.

God has already written the truth about grace and faith righteousness on our hearts, we just need to get our thinking straight to line up with the reality that is already in us. If you are a born again believer you do not have a spiritual problem, it's all mental

We must stop the insanity of trying to become what God has already made us to be. We are already righteous in Christ; we just need to awake to His righteousness, the only true righteousness of God which is by faith in Jesus.

CHAPTER 6

THE BORN IDENTITY

The number one theft in the world today is identity theft. If a thief can steal your identity he can ruin your credit and cause a lot of hardship, chaos and frustration to come into your life.

Many Christian's today live a very defeated, frustrated and even a spiritually bankrupt life that's full of chaos because the thief has made them blind to what God has already given them in Christ. Today, re-discover your new born identity in Christ and be free from the lies of the thief.

John 10:10

> *"The thief cometh not, but for to steal, and to kill, and to destroy: I am come that they might have life, and that they might have it more abundantly."*

Satan is a thief and one of the main things that

he is after is to steal your identify in Christ. Satan does not want us to know who we are in Christ, because he knows once we see this, it's game over for him.

Once we see our true identity in Christ the condemner can never condemn us again because we know that we have already been made to be the righteousness of God in Christ and that now there is now no condemnation for those in Christ. Once we awaken to our true identify in Christ we will see ourselves, righteous, holy and complete in Christ because as He is so are we now in this life.

It's as we see ourselves already complete in Christ that we can then cease from all our striving to become like what God has already made us to be in Christ and instead walk in the peace and rest that God has called us to walk in. Many Christians lack peace because they are still trying to become what God has already made them to be.

The quicker we can simply acknowledge and believe who we already are right now in Christ the quicker we will be able to effectively reach others for Christ.

Philemon 1:6
> "That the communication of thy faith may become effectual by the acknowledging of every good thing which is in you in Christ Jesus."

THE BORN IDENTITY

The most effective way for us to communicate our faith to the world is by agreeing with God about what He has already created us to be in Christ. The most ineffective way that we communicate our faith is to not be in agreement with who God says we are in Christ.

When the world looks at us, what do they see? Do they see a poor, struggling, condemned fearful person trying their best to become like Jesus? Or do they see a person who is full of life, joy, confidence, peace and rest?

When we ask the world to come to Jesus, what do they see that we are inviting them into? Do they see us inviting them into our fears, struggles and condemnation or into His rest? What did Jesus invite people to?

Matthew 11:28-30 (Amp)
> *"Come to Me, all you who labor and are heavy-laden and overburdened, and I will cause you to rest. [I will o ease and relieve and p refresh q your souls. Take My yoke upon you and learn of Me, for I am gentle (meek) and humble (lowly) in heart, and you will find rest (relief and ease and refreshment and recreation and blessed quiet) for your souls. For My yoke is wholesome (useful, t good—not harsh, hard, sharp, or pressing, but comfortable,*

I'M SAVED! NOW WHAT?

gracious, and pleasant), and My burden is light and easy to be borne."

Jesus invited people to a place of rest and peace, not more struggle. Maybe more people would be interested in receiving what we have if they saw that it is better than what they have.

It is only as we see our new "Born Identity" in Christ that we will ever experience lasting peace and rest for our souls.

2 Corinthians 5:17 AMP
"Therefore if any person is engrafted in Christ (the Messiah) he is a new creation (a new creature altogether); the old previous moral and spiritual condition has passed away. Behold, the fresh and new has come!"

If you are born again, you may look the same outside but you are not the same inside! You are a brand new creation in Christ, the old you has been done away in the flesh and new has come. You, right now, are righteous and complete in Christ. This is your new identification. As we believe who God says we are in Christ, we will walk in true rest and peace.

We must agree with our new true "Born Identity." The old really has been done away and the new has come and is of God.

Today, in your Spirit, and in the sight of God,

you are as righteous as Jesus is, because you are in Him. Not only that, you have been joined with Him and have been made to be one with Him so, as He is so are we in this life.

Is Jesus struggling to be like the Father? Is Jesus struggling to be righteous or holy? Is Jesus trying to earn His way into the Kingdom of God? Absolutely not! He's already there! Jesus is sitting at the right hand of the Father right now and guess where the Bible says we as believers are right now in Christ? We are seated together with Him because we are now in Him. We must renew our minds to the truth of how God sees us right now in Christ if we are going to cease from all our struggles and enter His rest.

Ephesians 2:5-6
> *"Even when we were dead in sins, hath quickened us together with Christ, (by grace ye are saved;) And hath raised us up together, and made us sit together in heavenly places in Christ Jesus:"*

We are already sitting in heavenly places in Christ. This is our new present reality. In God's eyes I've already arrived! I'm not trying to get there by my works. By grace God has already made me to be there. Why would God do this? The next verse tells us why.

I'M SAVED! NOW WHAT?

Ephesians 2:7-9

> *"That in the ages to come he might show the exceeding riches of his grace in his kindness toward us through Christ Jesus. For by grace are ye saved through faith; and that not of yourselves: it is the gift of God: Not of works, lest any man should boast."*

We need to just stop all our religious struggles of trying to become what God has already made us to be. We don't need to do anything to become who we already are. In Christ we have arrived! As we believe this, grace takes what is already a reality on the inside and begins to manifest it through our bodies to the rest of the seen world. We must agree with our new "Born Identity" which is in Christ.

Remember the movie <u>The Bourne Identity</u>? Jason Bourne, because of trauma inflicted to his body, developed a condition called amnesia or a loss of memory. Jason forgot who he was.

Jason Bourne began to discover skills that he didn't realize he had. Jason Bourne also had an apartment, wealth, even a Swiss bank account filled with money and passports! Jason slowly begins to re-discover who is by the reading and studying of certain documents about him.

Wouldn't it be frustrating to not know who you are? What if we all had a secret identity that we hadn't yet figured out? I love this movie, because the whole movie is about a guy re-discovering who he already was and rediscovering skills that he already possessed.

Many Christians are like Jason Bourne. They have spiritual amnesia. They still do not know who God has already made them to be in Christ and they do not know the skills that God has already given them to walk in. Many Christians live a lot of frustration trying to be what God has already created them in Christ to be. Did you know that God has already created us in Christ and already equipped us with special skills for His glory?

Ephesians 2:10
> *"For we are God's workmanship, created in Christ Jesus to do good works, which God prepared in advance for us to do?"*

There is one scene in <u>*The Bourne Identity*</u> that I love and felt the Lord draw my attention to. It was a scene where Jason is on a train and looking at his own reflection in the window. He doesn't say it, but you can hear him think it. "Who am I?"

The Bible is really more of a mirror than a manual. The Bible is God's way to show us Who He really is and who He created us to be. As we look into the mirror of the word, we begin to re-discover who we really are in Christ. We see that we are already approved by God because of Jesus and we are healed from our spiritual amnesia.

2 Corinthians 3:18
> *"But we all, with open face beholding as in a glass the glory of the Lord, are changed into the same image from glory to glory, even as by the Spirit of the Lord."*

The Bible is the mirror given to us by God that reflects our true self in Christ. As we believe the image we see then we are transformed from the inside our by the grace of God

When Adam fell in the garden he bumped his head and developed a condition called spiritual amnesia. Man forgot who he was and why he was created. God, through His word and the Spirit, heals our spiritual amnesia so we may rediscover both who we really are and who He created us to be.

CHAPTER 7

THE KEY TO VICTORIOUS LIVING

Romans 7:14-25 (Amplified Bible)
"We know that the Law is spiritual; but I am a creature of the flesh [carnal, unspiritual], having been sold into slavery under [the control of] sin. For I do not understand my own actions [I am baffled, bewildered]. I do not practice or accomplish what I wish, but I do the very thing that I loathe [[b]which my moral instinct condemns]. Now if I do [habitually] what is contrary to my desire, [that means that] I acknowledge and agree that the Law is good (morally excellent) and that I take sides with it. However, it is no longer I who do the deed, but the sin [principle] which is at home in me and has possession of me.

I'M SAVED! NOW WHAT?

For I know that nothing good dwells within me, that is, in my flesh. I can will what is right, but I cannot perform it. [I have the intention and urge to do what is right, but no power to carry it out.] For I fail to practice the good deeds I desire to do, but the evil deeds that I do not desire to do are what I am [ever] doing. Now if I do what I do not desire to do, it is no longer I doing it [it is not myself that acts], but the sin [principle] which dwells within me [[c]fixed and operating in my soul]. So I find it to be a law (rule of action of my being) that when I want to do what is right and good, evil is ever present with me and I am subject to its insistent demands. For I endorse and delight in the Law of God in my inmost self [with my new nature]. But I discern in my bodily members [[d]in the sensitive appetites and wills of the flesh] a different law (rule of action) at war against the law of my mind (my reason) and making me a prisoner to the law of sin that dwells in my bodily organs [[e]in the sensitive appetites and wills of the flesh]. O unhappy and pitiable and wretched man that I am! Who will release and deliver me from [the shackles of] this body of death? O thank God! [He will!]

THE KEY TO VICTORIOUS LIVING

Through Jesus Christ (the Anointed One) our Lord! So then indeed I, of myself with the mind and heart, serve the Law of God, but with the flesh the law of sin."

I believe that in this Romans 7:14-25 passage, Paul is encouraging all who are born again Christians to live by the Spirit and not by our own fleshly self willpower. Many in church today have actually excluded the Holy Spirit from their theology, and because of this exclusion we see a lot of struggling Christians doing their utmost best to live for God. Most in church today are actually told that they need to just keep trying harder to live for God or they just need to get the latest "how to live for God" book and try harder to do it. But this self willpower theology will never work. It only keeps them in a continuous vicious cycle of temporary victories but mostly defeat. It didn't work before they were saved, and it will not work after they are saved. We cannot live for God by sheer willpower.

Now in Romans 7, the flesh is not talking about the old Adamic nature, but the mortal body that was corrupted by the old nature. We cannot live for God by the flesh. We cannot live for God by sheer willpower, by just trying harder or how- to books, recommitments, or new resolutions. The law of sin in our body, like gravity, will sooner or later cause us to eventually fall.

In verse 22, Paul lets us know that we may

delight in the law of God in the inward man or the new nature, but because of this other law that still exists in our members or mortal body; it will not allow us to do what we desire to do in the inward man. In verse 24, Paul finally makes a point by shouting out, "O wretched man that I am! Who then will deliver me from this body of death?" Or how can I stop this vicious up and down cycle of victory and defeat? The answer to this struggle of trying and failing is to stop trying to live for God by the flesh and sheer willpower. Instead, surrender by faith to the One inside of you Who is the Spirit. We don't live for God, we live from God. It is God Who is at work inside of us both to will and to do His good pleasure. It takes faith to just surrender to the Holy Spirit, to believe that He is the One that will do the living, not you! The answer to living a victorious Christian life is to stop trying to live the victorious Christian life. Quit buying all the "how to live for God" books, and just know that God is at work in you to lead you and guide you into victorious living.

How many Christians today live more of a Romans 7 defeated, condemned way of life, instead of a Romans 8 way of life, of peace and no condemnation? Sad to say, most live more of the Romans 7 way than the Romans 8 way because of where their focus is. In Romans 7, the word "I" is mentioned over 30 times and "spirit" only once! But in Romans 8, it's reversed! "Spirit" is mentioned 19 times and "I" only twice!

THE KEY TO VICTORIOUS LIVING

The key to our victory is where our attention is. Is our attention on "I", trying my best to live for God, or is our attention on the Spirit of Christ Who lives in me? Paul says it best in Galatians 2:20:

"I have been crucified with Christ [in Him I have shared His crucifixion]; it is no longer I who live, but Christ (the Messiah) lives in me; and the life I now live in the body I live by faith in (by adherence to and reliance on and complete trust in) the Son of God, Who loved me and gave Himself up for me."

You will never find your real purpose in this life until you see yourself first in Christ.

CHAPTER 8

FREE TO BE YOU

God wants you free to be you. There is no better person that you can be than the unique you that God created you to be. You are not the invention of your parents. Your arrival may have been a big surprise to them but not to God. You were fearfully and wonderfully made by God for a distinct and unique purpose.

Psalm 139:14
> "I will praise thee; for I am fearfully and wonderfully made: marvelous are thy works; and that my soul knows right well."

When God made you, He made you for a special purpose.

Jeremiah 1:5 AMP
> "Before I formed you in the womb I knew

and approved of you as My chosen instrument, and before you were born I separated and set you apart, consecrating you; and I appointed you as a prophet to the nations."

A Prophet is one who is called to bring a message and to represent God in the earth. We have not all been called to be prophets like Jeremiah, but we have all been called to bring a certain message and to re-present God in this earth. It is in Christ that we begin to discover who we really are and why we are here on planet earth. We also begin to discover what God has specifically called us to do.

As we renew our minds to the truth of God's word and confess truth (that is to agree with God's word even over our own feelings) we will begin to know God's full purpose for our lives.

Renew simply means to renovate, as you would renovate a house. When a house is renovated the old material is taken out and new put back into its place. To renew our minds means that we surrender our old thoughts and opinions for God's thoughts and opinions. God's thoughts about us are really the only thoughts that matter. His thoughts are higher than our thoughts and His ways our ways. Our thoughts will often lie to us telling us things that keep us from God and all He has purposed for our lives. Isaiah 55 gives us powerful insight about forsaking our thoughts for God's thoughts and the incredible result that comes as we do.

Isaiah 55:7-13 ESV

> *"Let the wicked forsake his way, and the unrighteous man his thoughts; let him return to the LORD, that he may have compassion on him, and to our God, for he will abundantly pardon. For my thoughts are not your thoughts, neither are your ways my ways, declares the LORD. For as the heavens are higher than the earth, so are my ways higher than your ways and my thoughts than your thoughts."*

Our thoughts will often tell us that God is against us, is angry with us, or does not care about us. Our thoughts will often tell us things like God could never forgive us for what we did in our past. These are the thoughts that God is telling us to forsake! Forsake all these condemning thoughts. These thoughts are not coming from God. God says that He is more than ready to love you, to have compassion on you. He is ready to not only forgive you but to abundantly forgive you! As we believe and receive God's thoughts over our own thoughts we will see God's abundant fruit begin to grow in our lives.

Isaiah 55:12-13 ESV

> *"For you shall go out in joy and be led forth in peace; the mountains and the hills before you shall break forth into*

> *singing, and all the trees of the field shall clap their hands. Instead of the thorn shall come up the cypress; instead of the brier shall come up the myrtle; and it shall make a name for the LORD, an everlasting sign that shall not be cut off."*

The result of believing God's thoughts over our thoughts will produce incredible results. We will begin to experience the manifestation of His kingdom in our lives. The Bible says the kingdom of God is righteousness, peace and joy in the Holy Ghost. God desires for us to go out in joy and be led in His peace but we must be willing to surrender our thoughts for His thoughts.

Much of the world, and sad to say much of the church today, is not partaking of all that God desires to give to them because of wrong thinking.

Many of our thoughts are formed from our culture, how we were raised or what we have been told or led to believe. Even at an early age, many are told they were no good and would amount to nothing. As we receive these thoughts we begin to form certain opinions about ourselves that are not necessarily true. These wrong thoughts have often led to depression which often led many to engage in hurtful addictions in an attempt to ease the pain of their wrong thoughts. Again, if we will begin to choose what God really thinks about us and how God sees us now, in Christ, we will be set free from all evil imaginations that have keep us bound in despair.

Jeremiah 29:11 ESV

> *"For I know the plans I have for you, declares the LORD, plans for welfare and not for evil, to give you a future and a hope."*

God knows the plans that He has for each of us. His plan is not to hurt you but to bless you, to give you a hope and a future. Paul tells us in Romans 12 that our lives will radically be transformed as we will choose to think differently, exchanging our thoughts for God's thoughts and God's thoughts are found in His word.

Romans 12:2 AMP

> *"Do not be conformed to this world (this age), fashioned after and adapted to its external, superficial customs, but be transformed (changed) by the entire renewal of your mind by its new ideals and its new attitude, so that you may prove for yourselves what is the good and acceptable and perfect will of God, even the thing which is good and acceptable and perfect in His sight for you."*

For us to renew our minds to the truth, we must not approach the Bible as a rule book but as a mirror. The Bible is really not a manual; it is about Emmanuel, which means God is with us. In the Old

Covenant God was with His people but now under the New Covenant God is more than with us, He is now in us.

Again the Apostle Paul tells us in Galatians about our new identity in Christ.

Galatians 2:20 ESV
> *"I have been crucified with Christ. It is no longer I who live, but Christ who lives in me. And the life I now live in the flesh I live by faith in the Son of God, who loved me and gave himself for me."*

As we see ourselves in Christ, and one with Christ, we will not only discover our purpose in life but we will also be supernaturally changed by the grace of God from the inside out. It is through this process of receiving, believing and seeing ourselves the way God sees us that we will find our security and true identity. We will also experience freedom, joy and peace that we could never obtain through our own independent ways of trying to find it ourselves apart from God.

Let me make it clear. You will never find your real purpose in this life until you see yourself first in Christ. We must exchange our thoughts for God's thoughts and God's ways for His ways.

We should never fall into the trap of comparing ourselves with others and trying to be like them. There is no better person we can be than who God created us to be. God designed us and wants to work specifically through the unique person that He created us to be.

The main reason Jesus came was to give His life for you, so He could to give His life to you, so that He could live His life in you and through you as you.

> We are now under a brand New Covenant established on better promises.

CHAPTER 9

FROM THE LAW WAY TO THE GRACE WAY

The law is holy and just, but the law, which included the "Big 10," could never make us righteous or holy before God. The law had one weakness and that weakness was us! Our weak flesh could not keep the law.

Romans 8:3-4 NET

> *"For God achieved what the law could not do because it was weakened through the flesh. By sending his own Son in the likeness of sinful flesh and concerning sin, he condemned sin in the flesh, so that the righteous requirement of the law may be fulfilled in us, who do not walk according to the flesh but according to the Spirit."*

I'M SAVED! NOW WHAT?

To live according to the flesh is to continue to strive in order to measure up to God through self effort and self determination. To live according to the Spirit means to rest in His righteousness which is righteousness that comes through faith in Jesus and the finished work of the cross. As we rest we simply respond to the leadership of the Holy Spirit in our lives. Again, we are not led by rule books or how to books, but by the Spirit of grace that now abides in us.

Hebrews 7:19
> *"For the law made nothing perfect, but the bringing in of a better hope did ; by the which we draw nigh unto God."*

The law is perfect but the law could never make anyone perfect. The bringing in of a better hope did make us perfect and that better hope is Jesus! Today we are not made perfect through our own self effort. We are made perfect by the blood of Jesus. Today, through the new birth, God has made us to be one with Christ so that everything He is, we now have become and we are now complete in Him.

The devil knows why the law was given, so the devil's ultimate deception was to take the law (which is good, holy and perfect) and use it to keep much of the church bound in a vicious cycle of sin, self effort and condemnation. He knows the only way for the church to be free from sin and condemnation is for the church to become dead to the law and alive to Christ, so he has kept them instead alive to the law which in turn renders Christ of no affect in their lives.

The law is good and the law is holy, but the law was never, never, never given to justify us or make us righteous before God.

Today we need to understand that we are no longer under any of the Old Covenant law at all, which includes the law written in stone that was called the ministry of death and condemnation. We are now under a brand New Covenant established on better promises. In fact, today we are to see ourselves dead to the law and married only to Christ.

Romans 7:4
> *"So, my brothers and sisters, you also died to the law through the body of Christ, so that you could be joined to another, to the one who was raised from the dead, to bear fruit to God."*

The fact is we will never bear real fruit unto God until we see ourselves fully dead to the law and joined to the Lord.

1 Corinthians 6:17
> *"But he that is joined unto the Lord is one spirit. Today we are married to Christ and not the law."*

To go back into a relationship with the law is to

commit spiritual polygamy. We are not married to both the law and Christ. We are either married to one or the other but not both. To be married to Christ is far better than being married to the law. If we choose to go the law way then it is an all or nothing deal. We must keep all the law or be guilty of all the law

James 2:10
> *"For whoever keeps the whole law but fails in one point has become accountable for all of it."*

Paul use to be a law man until he met Christ. Then Paul became a grace man! I believe the Message translation does a great job in the book of Galatians expressing the radical change that took place in the life of Paul when he finally came to the end of all his law ways and surrendered to grace.

Galatians 2:19-21 MSG
> *"What actually took place is this: I tried keeping rules and working my head off to please God, and it didn't work. So I quit being a "law man" so that I could be God's man. Christ's life showed me how, and enabled me to do it. I identified myself completely with him. Indeed, I have been crucified with Christ. My ego is no longer central. It is no longer important that I appear righteous before*

you or have your good opinion, and I am no longer driven to impress God. Christ lives in me. The life you see me living is not "mine," but it is lived by faith in the Son of God, who loved me and gave himself for me. I am not going to go back on that. Is it not clear to you that to go back to that old rule-keeping, peer-pleasing religion would be an abandonment of everything personal and free in my relationship with God? I refuse to do that, to repudiate God's grace. If a living relationship with God could come by rule-keeping, then Christ died unnecessarily."

The Apostle basically said, "As far as the law goes, I've been there done that and I refuse to go back to the law!" Paul was saying there is really only one way forward and it's called grace. To go back to the law of self achievement for righteousness is to fall from grace. To turn back to the law is to go in the wrong direction and will always lead to a dead end street.

The Apostle Paul said that he had to let go of his ego and choose to rest in the finished work of Jesus.

This actually reminded me of a silly waffle commercial where someone has a tight bulldog grip on their waffle saying, "Let go of my Eggo!" Whether we admit it or not, our own "ego" is one of the main reasons we do not want to rest in the finished work of the cross for righteousness. Our flesh often wants to receive glory for doing something to earn right standing with God. It is very clear in Scripture that no flesh will ever glory for what Christ has already accomplished for us and in us.

1 Corinthians 1:29-31
> *"That no flesh should glory in his presence. But of him are ye in Christ Jesus, who of God is made unto us wisdom, and righteousness, and sanctification, and redemption: That, according as it is written, He that glorieth, let him glory in the Lord."*

Religion often teaches that in order to be righteous and holy that we must dress a certain way, or do a certain amount of things in order to achieve holiness or righteousness before God. This is not what the Scripture teaches. The Bible says that God made us to be wisdom, holy, righteous and redeemed through the cross and by baptizing us into Christ. Again, as we were joined to the Lord all that He is we became and this was an act of grace so that no flesh can ever glory or take credit for what God has accomplished for us in Christ.

When we get to heaven, it will not be, "Glory be to Jesus and me." It will only be, "Glory be to the One who sits on the throne! He alone is worthy of all praise!"

We can never mix any of the law with grace. This unholy mixture will always frustrate grace and make Christ of no affect in the life of the believer. The Bible says that we are to be dead to the law and married to Christ. (Romans 7:4) To mix law with grace will only frustrate grace from working in the heart and life of the believer.

Galatians 2:21 AMP
> *"Therefore, I do not treat God's gracious gift as something of minor importance and defeat its very purpose; I do not set aside and invalidate and frustrate and nullify the grace (unmerited favor) of God. For if justification (righteousness, acquittal from guilt) comes through observing the ritual of the Law, then Christ (the Messiah) died groundlessly and to no purpose and in vain. His death was then wholly superfluous."*

Now, today there are those who often say that those who preach grace are against the law, but this is far from the truth. We who preach the New Covenant of grace are not against the law. We are for the law for the reason the law was given. The law was given to bring us to an end of fleshly striving for justification and to point us to fully place our complete faith in Jesus Christ and the finished work of the cross.

Because many do not understand grace and the function of grace, they often bring the law back in after salvation by saying, "The law is not for salvation, but the law is our moral compass. The law shows us how to live and what we are to do." What they fail to see is that we do not need external laws or rules for a moral compass. We don't even need the latest how to book for our moral compass or to show us how to live the Christian life. Today we have a new way of living. This new way is called the grace way! And grace is the Spirit of Christ that now lives in us to change us and direct us from the inside out. The New Covenant is all about an inside out work. Those who are the sons of God are led by the Spirit of God. God's Spirit, and not the law, is the new way we are to be led and transformed.

2 Corinthians 3:18
> *"But we all, with open face beholding as in a glass the glory of the Lord, are changed into the same image from glory to glory, even as by the Spirit of the Lord."*

The law and following external rules actually stunts spiritual growth. This is why there is so much immaturity in the church today. Many today are still trying to live the Christian life by the law of self effort instead of grace.

CHAPTER 10

THE KINGDOM OF GOD AND GRACE

God wants to move us to a new center, from self centeredness to God centeredness. Before the fall, man was God centered. After the fall, man moved to a new center of self. Man still believes that the entire world revolves around him. God's trinity is Father, Son and the Holy Ghost, not me, myself and I.

When we are born again, we are born from above, born of the Spirit. But being born again is not the end for why Jesus came, it's only the beginning.

Because of our old self centered mentality, we have often made salvation the end of what Jesus came for when really it's just the beginning. There is much more to the Christian life than getting saved and getting our ticket to heaven.

God has really called us to a bigger eternal purpose called His kingdom. Jesus preached the good news of the kingdom of God everywhere that He went. The Bible says that Jesus came to prepare a kingdom for the Father and that the end will come when He delivers this kingdom to the Father. (1 Corinthians 15:24)

The kingdom of God speaks of the big picture, the eternal purpose and intention of God. The kingdom of God is the above the line eternal purpose of God. The way that this purpose is fulfilled is going to be in an above the line way and not in a below the line way.

Above the line speaks of the eternal unseen spirit realm and below the line speaks of temporary seen flesh realm. Babel is an example of men trying in a fleshly, carnal way of trying to build a kingdom for God.

Genesis 11:4
> *"And they said, Go to, let us build us a city and a tower, whose top may reach unto heaven; and let us make us a name, lest we be scattered abroad upon the face of the whole earth."*

Man has always had a tendency to organize, build and make a name for himself in his kingdom building efforts for God. But Jesus gives us the true above the line way of doing the will of God and seeing God's kingdom fulfilled.

John 5:19

> "Jesus answered them by saying, I assure you, most solemnly I tell you, the Son is able to do nothing of Himself (of His own accord); but He is able to do only what He sees the Father doing, for whatever the Father does is what the Son does in the same way in His turn."

Jesus did not move independently from the Father trying to build stuff for Him. Jesus did not move and do things by the flesh. His eyes were on the Father and Jesus simply responded and did whatever He was shown by the Father. Jesus was not anxiously trying to figure out what He should do next. Jesus did not feel that He had to stay busy for the Father or the Father would be displeased with Him. Yet, Jesus accomplished more than any human had ever accomplished and most of it was accomplished in 3 short years. Do you think that maybe we should stop all our religious busy activity and learn from Him?

John 21:25

> "And there are also many other things which Jesus did, the which, if they should be written every one, I suppose that even the world itself could not contain the books that should be written. Amen."

I'M SAVED! NOW WHAT?

How did Jesus do all of these things? It's called resting, relying and responding. Jesus walked in rest, Jesus relied on the Father and Jesus simply responded to what the Father was showing Him to do. He now calls us to do the same.

Matthew 11:28-30 MSG
> *"Are you tired? Worn out? Burned out on religion? Come to me. Get away with me and you'll recover your life. I'll show you how to take a real rest. Walk with me and work with me—watch how I do it. Learn the unforced rhythms of grace. I won't lay anything heavy or ill-fitting on you. Keep company with me and you'll learn to live freely and lightly."*

The Bible says that in Him we now live and move and have our being. The same way Jesus did it is how we are to do it. God's kingdom will not come by carnally trying to build by doing a lot of stuff for God. No! It comes by simply moving into what the Father shows us to do step by step. It comes as we walk after the Spirit, not the flesh. Someone asked once. "How do you walk in the Spirit?" That's simple, you do it one step at a time. Walking in the Spirit is much like trying to walk naturally. When a baby first learns to walk he is always watching his feet and concentrates on every step that he takes, but after a while the baby will not even notice that his feet are moving. He will

THE KINGDOM OF GOD AND GRACE

just walk. This is how we walk in the Spirit. It is a process that we learn. It's a process of resting and responding to what God shows us to do.

Now for us to even begin to participate in God's kingdom we must first be born from above.

John 3:5-6
> *"Jesus answered, Verily, verily, I say unto thee, Except a man be born of water and of the Spirit, he cannot enter into the kingdom of God. That which is born of the flesh is flesh; and that which is born of the Spirit is spirit."*

For us to even participate in the kingdom of God we must be born twice; once of the flesh and then once of the Spirit. It's interesting to note that Jesus was speaking to a very religious man named Nicodemus when he made the statement, you must be born again.

Being engaged in a lot of religious works does not necessarily mean that you have been born again. Nicodemus was probably more devoted in doing more for God then most Christians today. Good works is not what saves us, Jesus and faith in Him is what saves us, and it's through faith in Christ that we are born from above.

The only way we can become involved in kingdom above activity is to be born again or born from above. It is only by the Spirit that we are ever enabled to do kingdom activity, not the flesh.

I'M SAVED! NOW WHAT?

Galatians 5:25
> *"If we live in the Spirit, let us also walk in the Spirit."*

We are also enabled to participate in the kingdom of God as we are moved from a place of dead works to rest and faith. Dead works are all those works that you do still trying to earn or maintain favor with God. True faith says God is already pleased with me. It's not because of my works but because of the finished work of a Jesus. As we move from dead work activity we will be able to enter in the rest that God has already prepared for us. Out of His rest we will then be able to move in good works. We will also be moved from condemnation to confidence toward God.

Romans 8:1 says that there is now no more condemnation for those who are in Christ who walk not after the flesh but after the Spirit. When Paul mentions flesh here he is not just speaking of that yucky sinful flesh but the U.S.D.A. that we often put our confidence in trying to do great works for God or to obtain favor with God.

God does not want us in condemnation. Condemnation will only keep us self focused, self centered and only keep us in full time ministry to ourselves. On the other hand confidence toward God will move us from a place of self centeredness to Christ centeredness and rest. In confidence we will then be able to see and hear what the Father is saying and showing us to do. It is almost virtually impossible to walk in the Spirit and walk in condemnation at the same time. This is why the enemy loves to promote theology that is laced with condemnation.

One of the greatest needs for the church today is to get delivered from bad theology that breeds condemnation in the life of the believer.

As we are delivered from condemnation and self focused ministry, we will then be free to know what it means to seek first the kingdom of God which is the bigger plan and His righteousness. We will begin to realize that our being saved was not the end goal but really just the beginning to entering into the bigger plan of God which is to participate in His kingdom.

Even as I am writing these things, I just felt the Lord say, "Rick you're not writing, you are simply taking notes for me." The Bible was not written by educated men but it was written as they were moved by the Spirit on what to write. This is what it means to participate in the kingdom.

2 Peter 1:20-21

"Knowing this first, that no prophecy of the scripture is of any private interpretation. For the prophecy came not in old time by the will of man: but holy men of God spake as they were moved by the Holy Ghost."

But we need to understand that salvation is not the end but the beginning of what God has called us

I'M SAVED! NOW WHAT?

to. He has called us to participate with Him in His kingdom being expressed on earth as it is in Heaven.

Here is a good illustration of what we are saying. A certain man had a chance to obtain a very limited ticket to the Big Super Bowl game and in fact someone that loved the man had actually purchased a ticket and then gave the ticket to the man for the big game. After the man receives the ticket he becomes so excited about having the ticket and showing His ticket to everyone in the parking lot that he actually winds up missing the entire game.

The man missed the entire reason for having a ticket in the first place and that was to get him into the game. This is how so many Christians are today. We often think that Jesus came to just give us a ticket for heaven and we have made the ticket the ultimate end when instead the ticket was really a way to get us into the game. The ticket was not only to get us into heaven one day but the ticket was also a way for is to enter into seeing and participating in the game. The big game being the kingdom of God.

Again our very first step is to be born again to get our ticket so that we then may be able to enter into active participation of the eternal purpose of God which is His kingdom.

Matthew 5:20 AMP
> *"For I tell you, unless your righteousness (your uprightness and your right standing with God) is more than that of*

> *the scribes and Pharisees, you will never enter the kingdom of heaven."*

Religion will not get us into the game. Works toward righteousness will not give us access into the kingdom of God. We can't even see the game if we are busy in dead works. Salvation is just the beginning and not the end of seeing Gods kingdom purpose fulfilled.

Now once we have our ticket it's time to enter into the game where we will not only see the game being played out but we will actually participate in the game itself. But to effectively participate, we must be careful of distractions all around us in the stands. Jesus speaks of some of these distractions.

Matthew 6:31-33
> *"Therefore do not worry, saying, 'What shall we eat?' or 'What shall we drink?' or 'What shall we wear?' For after all these things the Gentiles seek. For your heavenly Father knows that you need all these things. But seek first the kingdom of God and His righteousness, and all these things shall be added to you."*

God's kingdom and His righteousness are the top two priorities that God says we are to seek after in this life. Not things, not even food or clothes which are often seen as essentials in this life, but His kingdom is what we are to really seek. God says if we will seek these two things first then all the other things will be added to us. The question is, "Do we believe that God loves us enough to take care of all these other things if we will seek first what He has called us to seek?"

Unfortunately, most Christians never make these two things their top priority but instead, like much of the world, they are often caught up in seeking the other things first and if there is any time left over then we will then seek Gods kingdom. I am not writing this to bring condemnation on anyone. It really does take faith to trust that God knows what we have need of and that God will indeed will take care of all the other things as we seek first His kingdom and His righteousness. We need to trust that God knows what is best. Father knows best. God will never lead us into condemnation but always into liberation. For true freedom to come, we must often choose faith over what makes sense.

Did Jesus come to seek things? Or did Jesus come and seek to do the Fathers will? And as Jesus did the Fathers will not only were all His needs met but He always had plenty to meet the needs of others.

Often times we have seen the gospel turned into a way for us to now focus on and believe God for things. The "Everyone should have a Cadillac gospel." I'm not sure the reason Jesus came to die was so that everyone could drive a Cadillac but I do know He came that we might have life and have life more abundantly.

Don't get me wrong, I am not against having things. God has blessed me with a lot of nice things. I thoroughly enjoy all the things that God has given me. But I'm not sure if I should use the faith of Jesus to believe for a Cadillac. This is more of the name it claim it, take it home and frame it gospel.

But neither do I believe that every Christian should sell all their possessions and become homeless wanderers in order to be a disciple. To be honest, I don't even know any Christians that have actually done this. Even the ones who passionately preach the "Sell everything gospel" (that only heaps condemnation on those they preach to) have themselves not even done this. Some may ask, "Didn't Jesus tell us that we had to sell everything to follow Him?" No. He told the one rich ruler to do this because those things the young rich ruler possessed actually possessed him. It's ok to have things as long as things don't have us.

Matthew 19:21-22 NKJV
> *"Jesus said to him, "If you want to be perfect, go, sell what you have and give to the poor, and you will have treasure in heaven; and come, follow Me." But when the young man heard that saying, he went away sorrowful, for he had great possessions."*

And just a note, you don't have to be rich for

things to have you. You can also be poor and still be possessed by things. We have seen the hoarders who live in piles of stuff and most of it is garbage. Why do they do this? They do it because they think it gives them security and value. I have seen homeless people pulling and pushing loads of stuff all over town and have often thought, "Why are they holding on to all this stuff? It seems that they would be able to be able to move around a lot easier without all of this." But again, it gives a sense of security and value. We also who have homes with garages and storage sheds packed with stuff. Why in the world do we hang on to all of this stuff? Oh, I know, we might need it one day! Right!

For us to really be free we must keep the main thing the main thing, seek first the kingdom of God and His righteousness and then all these other things will be added to us. We must realize that salvation is just the very beginning and not the end. Salvation is our way into the game. We are not on planet earth just to believe God for things so that we can be comfortably until we die. Neither are we here to just be spectators. No, God wants us to experience the joyful participation of being involved in His Kingdom. We must remember that being involved in His kingdom is not a heavy yoke or burden. It is light and easy. (Matthew 11:28)

So again, what is the kingdom of God? The kingdom of God is the full expression of God. It is the nature of God, the ways of God and the will of

THE KINGDOM OF GOD AND GRACE

God. It is also the wisdom of God, the ultimate intention of God, and the revelation of God. It is the truth of God and the people of God. The kingdom of God is righteousness, joy and peace in the Holy Ghost. Being involved in the kingdom of God is by far the most exciting thing that you will ever be involved in.

We need to understand that there is far more to the Kingdom than what we have often been taught and faith and grace is how the Kingdom is realized

> We are no longer to try our best to live for God. We now live from God.

CHAPTER 11

THE KINGDOM OF GOD AND GRACE 2

The only way that we will ever effectively become involved in the kingdom of God is through grace. It is by grace that we accomplish all that God calls us to do.

It may surprise many to know that God's work only begins when we enter into His rest. God's work does not begin by our forging ahead trying to do a bunch of stuff for God. God's work is not by perspiration but by participation. Remember perspiration came as a result of the fall and the curse.

Genesis 3:19
> *"In the sweat of thy face shalt thou eat bread, till thou return unto the ground; for out of it wast thou taken: for dust thou art, and unto dust shalt thou return."*

I'M SAVED! NOW WHAT?

But under the New Covenant we are no longer under the curse but under grace. Under this New Covenant of grace, His yoke is easy and His burden is light. This is not to say that we will never roll up our sleeves again and go to work or that now we will all just sit around and become praise the Lord coach potatoes! It means that instead of doing things by the flesh we now have grace and Gods grace is how we now function. The Apostle Paul said this about work and grace.

1 Corinthians 15:10
"But by the grace of God I am what I am: and his grace which was bestowed upon me was not in vain; but I labored more abundantly than they all: yet not I, but the grace of God which was with me."

Notice Paul said I labor more than anyone but it was not me but grace that was with me. Today we must not rely on our flesh to do the works but grace. This is how Jesus did it and this is also how we are called to do it.

When Jesus came, He came full of grace and truth. All that Jesus accomplished in 3 short years was by grace. We will get a whole lot more accomplished by grace than we could ever do in a life time of planning and striving by the flesh.

It is by grace and faith that we will properly represent the kingdom of God in this earth.

THE KINGDOM OF GOD AND GRACE 2

Romans 5:17

> *"For if by one man's offense death reigned by one; much more they which receive abundance of grace and of the gift of righteousness shall reign in life by one, Jesus Christ."*

The way we begin to rule and reign in this life is by receiving not doing. As we receive both the abundance of grace and the free gift of righteousness, we will reign in this life by One, Jesus Christ. We reign in life because of the One, Who is now in us. Jesus, Who is full of grace and truth, now lives in us and so as He is we are in this life. When we received Jesus, we also received His fullness.

John 1:16

> *"And of his fullness have all we received, and grace for grace."*

Most in the church still do not understand how we are to function now in this life. We are no longer to try our best to live for God. We now live from God. God has, under the New Covenant, given us the fullness of Christ! Christ is now in us. So now the works He did I can now do and even greater works. So if this is true, why are we not seeing the works of Christ? The problem is located right between our own two ears. It has been a matter of wrong believing.

We have often taught only half the gospel and

with only half the gospel we will only get half the results. What do I mean by half the gospel? We have been taught that Jesus died on the cross for our sins, made us a new creation, forgave our sins and we now have our ticket for heaven. We haven't really been taught a very vital truth and that is how we live the Christian life or rather how now is this new Christ-in-me life is now manifested through me. We have not really been taught Galatians 2:19-21.

Galatians 2:19-21
> *"For I through the law am dead to the law, that I might live unto God. I am crucified with Christ: nevertheless I live; yet not I, but Christ liveth in me: and the life which I now live in the flesh I live by the faith of the Son of God, who loved me, and gave himself for me. I do not frustrate the grace of God: for if righteousness come by the law, then Christ is dead in vain."*

We have not been taught what it means to be dead to the law. We have not been taught what it really means to be crucified with Christ. We have not been taught what it means to have Christ now living in me as me.

What we have been taught is that we are forgiven, born again Christians that now need to do our utmost through trying real hard to live for God.

THE KINGDOM OF GOD AND GRACE 2

We have been taught that we need to do our best to keep the Law of Moses (you know the big 10) and that God really grades on a curve so as long as we keep trying real hard that we will be OK with God. We have also been taught that, yes, we are new creations in Christ but the old really has not been done way, we still possess an old nature. In other words, when Christ came in, He, in essence, is now roommates with the devil. What we have been taught is not the gospel of Christ. A partial gospel or a mixed gospel and our wrong belief have kept us, for the most part, wandering in the wilderness.

I'm reminded of what a good friend of mine, the late John Kellogg, wrote in His book *"A Kingdom for the Father"* that really grabbed my attention. He used Nehemiah 9:19-22 as the Scripture reference to his insight.

Nehemiah 9:19-21 NASB

>*"You, in Your great compassion, Did not forsake them in the wilderness; The pillar of cloud did not leave them by day, To guide them on their way, Nor the pillar of fire by night, to light for them the way in which they were to go. "You gave Your good Spirit to instruct them, Your manna You did not withhold from their mouth, And You gave them water for their thirst. "Indeed, forty years You provided for them in the wilderness and they were not*

in want; Their clothes did not wear out, nor did their feet swell."

John said as he read this, it dawned on him that this sounded strangely enough like the full gospel that we often preach today. Come to Jesus, He will deliver you. He will provide for you. He will take care of you until death. He will give you direction in life and all these things are true and benefits from knowing the Lord, but did you know that God had a higher purpose for them than to just take care of them in the wilderness? God had called them to possess the promise land which represents His kingdom purpose. Because God is merciful, even though His people were a very unbelieving and refused to go forward into what God had called them to do, He still took care of them.

Provision, healing and all these other things are incredible benefits that we receive for being a part of Gods family but God has not just saved us so we could have these things. He saved us and called us to a higher purpose, which involves His kingdom being expressed on earth as it is in heaven.

Such a gospel will leave us all dressed up with nowhere to go or without a purpose. Our purpose is not to just sit around on our blessed assurance and wait for Jesus to come back to rescue us from this present evil world. No, God has called us to be delivered from this present evil world, while we are living in it. He has called us to be a light in this dark world, to be the salt of the earth that will make people truly thirsty for God. We are called to be ambassadors for Christ, to not just represent Christ but to re-present Christ. We are called to express Christ in this world.

In order for this to happen it will not come by our trying harder or by trying to do better and be better. We already know that has not worked. It will not come by our buying the latest how to live the Christian life or how to do the Christian works book. These books are often top sellers, but for the most part, they still do not work.

You know the definition of insanity is to keep doing the same things and expect different results.

So what is the key to seeing us becoming fully engaged into the kingdom of God, if it's not trying harder? Well how about this! Why don't we try something new? Why don't we take a leap of faith! Why don't we, instead of trying harder, just make up our minds to stop all our trying and instead rest. A major key to seeing Gods kingdom advance in this world is entering into His rest. As we rest, God then works. As we begin to believe the truth of the whole gospel, not just the partial gospel or mixed gospel, we will see the power of the gospel released in and through the church.

> If we are in Christ and He is in us, we are more than qualified for full time ministry.

CHAPTER 12

GRACE QUALIFIES YOU FOR MINISTRY

I will never forget sitting in a church several years ago and a visiting evangelist asked the congregation. "Who here today is in full-time ministry?" Needless to say, the only one who raised his hand was the Pastor. But the true answer for this question is really, everyone who has ever been born again is also born into full time ministry.

So my question is this, "Have we actually disqualified many people from being engaged in full-time ministry by giving them the wrong impression or idea about what full-time ministry really is?"

Full-time ministry is not about a paid position in the church. Full-time ministry is not about a degree we earned in college, neither is it a title such as Pastor, Bishop, or Priest. Full-time ministry is about making ourselves available to the One who now lives in us.

I'M SAVED! NOW WHAT?

2 Corinthians 5:20 AMP
> "So we are Christ's ambassadors, God making His appeal as it were through us. We as Christ's personal representatives beg you for His sake to lay hold of the divine favor now offered you and be reconciled to God."

Every born again believer has been reconciled back to God, it's a done deal! Now God wants to make His appeal through us so that others may be reconciled to Him as we were. The way this effectively happens is when we lay hold of God's divine favor which is grace. Believe that He now lives in is and then yield to His promoting.

Romans 12:1 AMP
> "I APPEAL to you therefore, brethren, and beg of you in view of all the mercies of God, to make a decisive dedication of your bodies presenting all your members and faculties as a living sacrifice, holy (devoted, consecrated) and well pleasing to God, which is your reasonable (rational, intelligent) service and spiritual worship."

Presenting yourself as a living sacrifice to God is true ministry. Ministry is making yourself available to the One Who lives inside of you. Present yourself; make yourself available to Christ, to His ministry. We need to understand that all true ministry is His. It's not my ministry! It's His ministry! It's about Christ's life that God has placed in me now flowing through me out to others. This happens as we present ourselves to Him as a living sacrifice and we refuse to be conformed to this world and instead we renew our minds to the truth of the gospel. God's grace qualifies us for full-time ministry.

Every born again believer has true ministry in Christ, which means everyone is qualified and equipped for ministry.

Religion and self righteousness will disqualify you from ministry but grace will always qualify you for ministry. So many in churches today feel disqualified or unqualified for ministry. This is a lie that needs to be broken off the minds of believers. If we are in Christ and He is in us, we are more than qualified for full time ministry. Why? Because it's not about you it's about the One inside of you.

Jesus did something incredible when He rose from the dead; He became a life giving Spirit. Jesus duplicated Himself in the life of everyone that receives Him.

1 Corinthians 15:45 AMP

"Thus it is written, The first man Adam became a living being (an individual personality); the last Adam (Christ)

became a life-giving Spirit restoring the dead to life."

The Bible says that the same Spirit that raised Christ from the dead now lives in me.

Romans 8:11 AMP
"And if the Spirit of Him Who raised up Jesus from the dead dwells in you, then He Who raised up Christ Jesus from the dead will also restore to life your mortal (short-lived, perishable) bodies through His Spirit Who dwells in you."

Reconciliation is the gift that God has placed in every believer to reconcile people back to Himself. Every believer is qualified for true ministry. I don't care if you are one day old in the Lord or if you have been saved 50 years and have 10 degrees. True ministry is not about degrees or education it's about first is Christ in you? Do you believe Christ is in you? And are you available to Him? Are you willing to respond to whatever He says or what He prompts you to say and do?

Colossians 1:29
"Whereunto I also labour, striving according to his working, which works in me mightily."

GRACE QUALIFIES YOU FOR MINISTRY

I'm always amazed when people who knew I pastored a church for several years ask me why I got out of the ministry. This really has shown me that most today have no clue what true ministry is. Again, it's not about a title or position. It's not about a wooden thing called a pulpit! It's about Jesus in you, expressing Himself through the unique you as you walk around in your everyday life. If Christ is in you, you are qualified to be engaged in full-time ministry. I don't care if you're a farmer or a coffee shop owner, you take Jesus everywhere because He is in you.

I have probably ministered to more people as a coffee shop owner then I ever did in a church building. For one, I'm in the world. I'm in the market place. I'm where Jesus told us to go and shine the light!

Jesus did not tell the world to go into every church and hear the gospel. He told the church to go into the world and preach the gospel. He told us to go and shine!

Matthew 5:14

"Ye are the light of the world. A city that is set on an hill cannot be hid."

Remember the woman at the well? She immediately became engaged in full-time ministry and brought revival to an entire city. She was so excited; she could not help but tell people about Jesus. To be honest, what we need in more churches is more joy and less fear.

I'M SAVED! NOW WHAT?

So many people in church look like they have been baptized more in lemon juice than in grace. When you get a hold of God's grace it will fill you with peace and joy!

How did Jesus do ministry and how did Jesus say future believes would do ministry? Jesus was filled with the Spirit and He said that we too would be filled with the Spirit.

John 14:17

Even "he Spirit of truth; whom the world cannot receive, because it sees him not, neither knows him: but ye know him; for he dwells with you, and shall be in you."

God is working in me both to will and to do His good pleasure. Ministry is not about you trying to muster up the courage to give someone the four spiritual laws, it's about resting in and being confident that God is in you and He has given you the anointing and will give you the right words to speak to very one to meet every need. Ministry is not a formula we follow! Ministry is being led by the One in you. This is how Jesus did it and this is how we are to do it.

Education is good and it helps to renew our minds to who we are now in Him.. But too often men have leaned too much on what they know instead of who they know lives in them. We do not need a degree to be engaged in ministry.

GRACE QUALIFIES YOU FOR MINISTRY

Most of the early church including many of the apostles was uneducated; Peter, James and John were all uneducated fishermen. How did they do ministry. They did it by knowing what God had put in them, they did it by silver and gold I don't have but such as I have I give to you. The God of this world has blinded the hearts and minds of the world so they will not believe the truth. God wants to use us to open their blind eyes.

In true ministry we do not preach ourselves but Christ. Who is the center of our ministry? Is it me? Is it my denomination? Am I trying to get people into my brand name of church or into Christ? Are we trying to build a franchise or lead people to Christ? True ministry will make Christ the center.

1 Corinthians 1:12-17

> *"Now this I say, that every one of you saith, I am of Paul; and I of Apollos; and I of Cephas; and I of Christ. Is Christ divided? was Paul crucified for you? or were ye baptized in the name of Paul? I thank God that I baptized none of you, but Crispus and Gaius; Lest any should say that I had baptized in mine own name. And I baptized also the household of Stephanas: besides, I know not whether I baptized any other. For Christ sent me not to baptize, but to preach the gospel:*

not with wisdom of words, lest the cross of Christ should be made of none effect."

Which name are we focused on, our name, our church name or Christ? Who was crucified for us? We must keep Christ the center. All true ministry flows from Him.

1 Corinthians 3:9
> *"For we are laborers together with God: ye are God's husbandry, you are God's building."*

The church is not the building of God. We are God's building and we are all ministers together with God. Believe this, God is in you and wants to express Himself through you today.

CHAPTER 13

EMPOWERED BY GRACE

Living the Christian life without grace is not difficult it is impossible! We were never called to live the Christian life by our own human effort or strength. Living by soul power instead of Spirit power is not the way to live the Christian life.

Grace is God's Spirit enabling us to accomplish what we could never accomplish through our own human effort or ability. Grace is the power of God, the Spirit of God and the strength of God. I can do all things through Christ, Who strengthens me. That's grace.

Grace can only work as we cease from our own work and enter into rest. When we work, grace cannot work. When we rest, that's when grace can then effectively go to work.

We obtain grace and walk by grace through faith. It takes faith to believe that grace will work if we cease from all our works. It takes faith to enter into the rest of God.

Much of the church today begins in the Spirit but then winds up trying to live for God by the flesh. Paul calls this a foolish way. Much of the church is running on soul power and not Spirit power. Soul refers to our mind, will and emotions. Man is not just body and soul; he is body, soul and spirit. We are not to live and walk by the soul. As born again believers, the spirit and not the soul and body, is to take the lead in all that we do. When soul and body are leading instead of spirit this is called flesh. The only thing that flesh will produce apart from the spirit is just more flesh. It may be nice looking flesh but it will still be flesh

One of the main reasons that there is so much division and discord in the church today is due to the fact that we have tried to live the Christian life by the flesh instead of by grace, Who is the Spirit of Christ. A vital truth that we must understand is that grace is not a doctrine but grace is the Spirit of Christ that now lives in us. Grace is the way we live the Christian life. Grace is how Jesus accomplished all that He accomplished and grace is how we will accomplish all that God has called us to accomplish in this life.

John 1:12

"But as many as received him, to them gave he power to become the sons of God,

even to them that believe on his name:"

The power to become the sons of God is the grace of God.

John 1:14
"And the Word was made flesh, and dwelt among us, (and we beheld his glory, the glory as of the only begotten of the Father,) full of grace and truth."

John 1:16-17
"And of his fullness have all we received, and grace for grace. For the law was given by Moses, but grace and truth came by Jesus Christ."

Jesus came full of grace and truth and now every born again believer is full of grace and truth. The law came by Moses but grace and truth came by Jesus Christ.

Today we are not to try and live out the New Covenant Christian life in an Old Covenant way. The Old Covenant was about law. Under the old way it was man trying to keep the letter of the law through human effort and might. But under the New Covenant we have been given a new and better way to approach God and to carry out God's will on this earth. This new way to carry out God's will is called grace. Grace is not just for the forgiveness of sins but grace is what enables us and empowers us to do and to become all that God has called us to in this life.

Anytime someone says that you shouldn't preach to much grace because it will cause people to live a sinful reckless life, that person does not understand grace. You can never receive too much grace. In fact, grace is how we live out the Christian life. Without grace it's not only difficult to live the Christian life it is impossible! Jesus didn't do all that He did through human effort so what makes us think that we can?

Romans 5:17
> *"For if by one man's offense death reigned by one; much more they which receive abundance of grace and of the gift of righteousness shall reign in life by one, Jesus Christ.)"*

It is only as we receive the abundance of God's grace and the gift of righteousness that we will ever reign in life by One, Jesus Christ. How do we reign? We reign in life. Whose life, our life or the life of Jesus Christ? I'm reminded of the main reason Jesus came in this first place.

John 10:10
> *"The thief cometh not, but for to steal, and to kill, and to destroy: I am come*

that they might have life, and that they might have it more abundantly."

Abundant life is one of the main reasons Jesus came. Jesus did not come to give us more religion but Jesus came to give us abundant life and it is as we receive Gods abundant grace and free gift of righteousness that we begin to experience Christ's life in us. Jesus did not come to give us more law; He came to give us more life. He came to give us His abundant life.

The will of God for my life is to receive and to trust in grace to work in my life. I am to trust grace to lead me, to teach me, to guide me, to transform me.

Most of the controversy over grace today is a matter of trust. Most simply do not trust grace to do its full work or to bring to past what God has promised to do.

We are often like Abraham. If we do not see immediate results we try and help God out to make it happen. This helping God out is to move from faith to flesh. Grace does not work through flesh, grace only works through faith.

For grace to work we must stop trying to help God out! God knows how to bring to pass what He has promised and it is always in His time not ours. Either grace works or we work, but it's not both. For grace to work we must cease from all our own effort and enter into the rest of God.

I'M SAVED! NOW WHAT?

But will this not produce a bunch of lazy coach potato Christians? No! The believer who chooses to trust grace to work will accomplish more by accident than religion will ever accomplish on purpose.

Remember, Jesus did all He did because He stayed in rest and was full of grace. Today we are called to do it the same way that Jesus did it. Jesus now lives in us and wants to continue His ministry through us as we trust Him.

Jesus accomplished more than any human had ever accomplished in history, how did he do it? He was full of grace and He trusted grace to lead Him. Today we need to trust grace to work. We will accomplish far more by trusting grace than we could ever accomplish through human striving and wisdom.

John 21:25
> *"And there are also many other things which Jesus did, the which, if they should be written every one, I suppose that even the world itself could not contain the books that should be written. Amen."*

John 5:19 ESV
> *"So Jesus said to them, "Truly, truly, I say to you, the Son can do nothing of his own accord, but only what he sees the Father doing. For whatever the Father does, that the Son does likewise."*

Jesus only did what He saw the Father doing and what the Father was showing Him to do. Jesus did not do everything people told Him to do. Sometimes I wonder if we are being led more by what man is telling us to do than God.

As Jesus heard and saw what the Father was showing Him to do, He then responded and did what the Father was showing Him to do. Jesus simply rested and responded to the Father. We have got to move away from this "hurry up and get busy doing something for God" gospel.

Religion often tells us "Don't just stand there do something!" But grace says "Don't just do something stand there." We must first learn to stand and rest in Jesus before we can effectively do anything.

John 15:5

"I am the vine, ye are the branches: He that abides in me, and I in him, the same brings forth much fruit: for without me ye can do nothing."

Grace is not just for the initial salvation experience. Grace is how we are to do everything God has called us to. Grace enables us, empowers us, equips us and transforms us.

As we begin to trust grace we will be delivered from the hard, heavy yoke religious way of trying to live for God into the grace way that is light and easy. I love how The Message translation says it:

I'M SAVED! NOW WHAT?

Matthew 11:28-30

> *"Are you tired burned out on religion? come to me ,get away with me and you will recover your life. I will show you how to take a real rest. Walk with me and work with me-watch how I do it.. Learn the unforced rhythms of Grace. I will not lay anything heavy or ill- fitting on you. Keep Company with me and you will learn to live freely and lightly."*

CHAPTER 14

LIVING BY GRACE

Those who see grace as just basic Christianity 101 only for the initial Christian salvation experience do not really understand God's grace. We do not begin in grace and then move on from grace to bigger and better things. To think this way is deception and is actually a form of witchcraft. The Apostle Paul strongly rebuked the church in Galatia for this way of thinking.

Galatians 3:1-3
> "O foolish Galatians, who hath bewitched you, that ye should not obey the truth, before whose eyes Jesus Christ hath been evidently set forth, crucified among you? This only would I learn of you, Received ye the Spirit by the works of the law, or by the hearing of faith? Are ye so foolish? Having begun in the Spirit, are ye now made perfect by the flesh?"

Notice Paul again says it is foolish to move away from the truth of looking to the finished work of the cross (for righteousness) and also from relying on the Spirit (of grace) to a system of fleshly religious works for maturity and perfection.

One vital thing that we need to also understand here is that anytime the Bible mentions the word truth in the New Covenant, it is also speaking of Jesus and grace. Jesus, grace, and truth are always synonymous.

John 1:17
"For the law was given by Moses, but grace and truth came by Jesus Christ."

Notice it says that grace and truth came by Jesus Christ. Grace is truth and truth is grace and both truth and grace came by Jesus! To say that we should not preach too much grace is like saying that we shouldn't preach too much Jesus or truth.

Now again, we do not begin in grace for our initial salvation experience and then move on to some kind of religious system of self effort, rules and works of trying our best to then live for God and maintain our right standing with Him. We do not start out in grace and then perfect ourselves by the flesh! The Christian life is not about striving to maintain our right standing with God through good works. No! God is only pleased when we believe in what He has already provided through His Son Jesus!

LIVING BY GRACE

Isn't it amazing that before we were saved we knew that we could never do enough works to ever save ourselves, but now that we are saved we have been convinced that the only way we are able to maintain our right standing with God is by doing enough good works! The true Christian life is not about the works we do, but it's more about the grace that God has already given! We must understand that we could never accomplish enough or ever do enough good works to ever justify us or to put us in right standing with God before we were saved or after we are saved. Grace came to make us right and to keep us right before God.

Even though grace is a free gift from God, religion will always try it's best to move you from grace and into a system of works trying to earn your way with God. Religion works at keeping you bound in the fear of always wondering, "Am I doing enough to please God? Am I praying enough? Am I giving enough? Am I reading my Bible enough? Am I attending church enough? Am I doing enough? Am I doing enough? Am I doing enough?" In fact, most preaching today is centered around the big question of, "Are you doing enough to please God?"

But the true Christian life will set you free of all of these doubts and the fears of wondering, "Am I doing enough?" The true Christian life is really not about what I do as much as it is what has already been done through the One. The true Christian life is really about resting in what has already been done through the One, Jesus Christ! Because of the obedience of the One, Jesus Christ, we have already been given the free gift of righteousness and eternal life.

Romans 5:19 says:
> "For as by one man's disobedience many were made sinners, so by the obedience of one shall many be made righteous."

The true Christian life is really about keeping our eyes on the finished work of the cross for righteousness and relying on the Spirit of God's grace working in us to lead us and guide us into all truth and to transform us into His likeness from the inside out! 1 Peter 4:10 speaks of the manifold grace of God. God's grace is not elementary, neither is it just one sided. There are many sides to the grace of God. Grace is not just for the initial new birth. Grace is the way we as Christians are to now live, walk, grow, stand, and to do the entire work of the ministry. We never move on from grace to bigger and better things! Grace IS the big thing! In fact, it's the only thing. To move away from grace is to actually move away from Christ and into fleshly, carnal, dead religion.

Galatians 5:4
> "Christ is become of no effect unto you, whosoever of you are justified by the law; ye are fallen from grace."

LIVING BY GRACE

Today we often hear many preachers preaching against grace, even labeling those who preach too much grace as hyper-grace preachers, implying that if you preach too much grace then it will lead people to live a reckless life of sin and disobedience. Again, this is actually the opposite of what grace will do. In fact, the Bible says that the only way we can ever truly live free from the dominion of sin is by God's grace. You can never preach too much grace.

Romans 6:14

> "For sin shall not have dominion over you, for ye are not under the law, but under grace."

Romans 5:17

> "For if by one man's offense death reigned by one; much more they which receive abundance of grace and of the gift of righteousness shall reign in life by one, Jesus Christ."

When we move from grace to a "works/performance" mentality of pleasing God, we have not gone on to bigger and better things. We have actually fallen from grace and have gone backwards in our faith. We need to see grace as the jet fuel for the entire Christian life. Grace is like Miracle Grow for our Christian growth and maturity. Grace is how we are witnesses in this earth for

Christ. The Christian is not just saved by grace, we are to live by grace, we are to walk by grace, and we can really only grow in grace. The Christian can never grow in law or legalism or dead works. The Christian can only grow in grace. One of the main reasons we see so many immature Christians in the church today is due to the fact that they are under legalistic preaching and not grace.

2 Peter 3:18 says:
"But grow in grace, and in the knowledge of our Lord and Savior Jesus Christ."

Grace and the free gift of righteousness are what we must always look to God for and continue to receive in abundance every day. The only way to be victorious in this world that is full of lust, corruption, and deception is to continually be filled with the abundance of God's grace.

Galatians 4:1-2 says that those under law are kept bound in immaturity. We cannot grow in law and self effort. Law and self effort will only frustrate God's grace in our lives and stunt our growth and maturity in Christ.

Now, many today actually resist God's grace because it's not logical. It does not compute or make sense that as we cease from our own works, enter into God's rest, and continue to receive God's abundant grace that we will grow and mature. In the carnal mind we must do something to grow. It must somehow take some kind of self effort. But let me ask you a question, "How does a branch on a tree bear fruit? Does it do it through striving or simply relying and resting on the life that's in the tree?" A branch of a tree does not produce fruit through self effort, but by simply abiding in the vine who gives life to the branch to produce the fruit. Grace works when we stop working. As we abide in Christ and in the grace of God, we will produce effortless fruit.

The Bible says that it's when we leave grace and go back to our own self effort of trying and striving to please God, that's when we actually go backwards or backslide. Did you know that the true backslider isn't just the one who turns back to sin, but who turns back to the law of self effort of trying to please God by the flesh?

Galatians 5:4
> *"Christ is become of no effect unto you, whosoever of you are justified by the law; ye are fallen from grace."*

Grace is higher and greater than the law of self effort. We see this even in the shadow of the Old Covenant. For example, on top of the Ark of the Covenant was the mercy seat and beneath the mercy seat inside the ark was the law. So we see even in the ark that mercy and grace are higher than law and self. When you leave grace to legalistic religious self effort you actually fall from grace.

I'M SAVED! NOW WHAT?

Christianity is not a work of the flesh or self effort. It is a work of the Spirit and faith. Our flesh cannot produce fruit; only the Spirit can produce fruit.

Now we mentioned that there are many sides to grace, that grace has many functions. So let's look at some of the many functions of grace.

Grace is our teacher; it teaches us how to live Godly in this world.

Titus 2:11-13
> "For the grace of God that brings salvation hath appeared to all men, Teaching us that, denying ungodliness and worldly lusts, we should live soberly, righteously, and godly, in this present world; Looking for that blessed hope, and the glorious appearing of the great God and our savior Jesus Christ."

Grace is our helper to help us through in times of need.

Hebrews 4:16
> "Let us therefore come boldly unto the throne of grace, that we may obtain mercy, and find grace to help in time of need."

Notice it does not call God's throne a throne of judgment but a throne of grace!

LIVING BY GRACE

Hebrews 12:28

> *"Wherefore we are receiving a kingdom which cannot be moved, let us have grace, whereby we may serve God acceptably with reverence and godly fear."*

The only way we can serve God in an acceptable way is by grace.

> The Bible has to become more than a place to grace our coffee tables or hide our money.

CHAPTER 15

YOUR KEY TO SUCCESS

Proverbs 23:7 says:
"As a man thinks in his heart so is he."

I'm beginning to understand more and more that whatever goes on between our ears is the key to almost everything we receive and experience in this life from God. Our thinking is the key to manifesting all we have already been given by God in Christ. Our thinking is the key to our growth and maturity in Christ. Our thinking is the valve that either turns on or off the very life flow that God has put within us.

The Bible says that we are not to be conformed to this world but transformed by the renewing of our minds that we might be able to prove what is the good, perfect and acceptable will of God. The word of God reveals God's true nature and character. It reveals God's goodness and great love for us. The only thing that really stops us from experiencing the love and the life and the peace that God has for us is right between our ears.

The way we are transformed and experience everything that God has for us is through our minds, through our thought life. This is why it's so critical for us to not just casually read the Bible but to meditate on the word. To meditate means to rehearse over and over or to ponder on. Meditating on the word is critical for transformation. Now many might say, "I don't have time to meditate on the word" but that's not true! Whether you realize it or not, you are always meditating on something. Good or bad, you're always meditating or thinking about something. So meditating on the word is about choosing priorities.

Do you believe that simply meditating on the word and renewing your mind to the truth of God's word will really transform your life and manifest Gods abundance in you? It will, you just have to give it a chance to work.

Do we believe if we seek first the kingdom of God and His righteousness then all the other things will be added to us? Or are we too busy seeking first the things? Are we too busy trying to figure it all out for ourselves to meditate on God's word? God's word must take precedence in our lives. As we renew our minds to the promises of God in the word then we will be transformed and all things will be added to us. In fact, meditating on the word is the only way that we will ever have any true success in our lives.

YOUR KEY TO SUCCESS

Joshua 1:8

> *"This Book of the Law shall not depart out of your mouth, but you shall meditate on it day and night, that you may observe and do according to all that is written in it. For then you shall make your way prosperous, and then you shall deal wisely and have good success."*

As we meditate on the word of God and believe and do the things that the Holy Spirit show us to do, we will begin to make our way prosperous. We will have the wisdom we need to make the right decisions in life and we will have good success. But it says we are to meditate on the word day and night. In other words, we are to make God's word a priority in our lives!

We cannot expect to have a very prosperous life if we read the word like we would a fortune cookie, or if we just hear the word once a week in a church service! Once a week will make you weak! That would be like eating only once a week, it will not work. We must take in the word every day and meditate on the word.

Now don't get me wrong, God will still love you whether you read the Bible or not but reading and meditation of the word will help us in our daily life on this earth! I mean why spend all our lives poor, ignorant and defeated when the word will make our way prosperous.

I'M SAVED! NOW WHAT?

The Bible has to become more than a place to grace our coffee tables or hide our money. You know why the Bible is a good place to hide money? Because very few will open up the Bible and look in it.

Every Christian is responsible for his or her own growth in the Lord, especially today when we have plenty of access to the word of God. We can read the word, listen to the word and see the word in so many different ways. We have more access to God's word today than we have ever had since the world began through radio, TV, internet, CD's, and now even on our iPhones. I mean we really have no excuse not to get into the word. When people say, "I don't have time to read or meditate on the word" that's just not true. It's a matter of priority. We must make reading and meditating on God's word a priority if we are going to see all that God has for us manifest in our lives!

The word changes our thinking and as our thinking changes and begins to line up with God's word we will begin to experience the life and peace that God has for us. Your mindset will determine your life-set. So what are we meditating on? What are we thinking about?

Did you know to worry is to meditate on things that you should not be meditating on? I don't care what it is or what the circumstance is. If we begin to worry and become fearful we are meditating on the wrong things. Worry will not take care of one problem. This is why Jesus told us not to even go there!

YOUR KEY TO SUCCESS

Matthew 6: 27

> *"And who of you by worrying and being anxious can add one unit of measure (cubit) to his stature or to the [w]span of his life?"*

Worry is just a distraction from God's word and His kingdom. Why waste time in worry when you could be using that time to meditate on God's word.

Matthew 6:33-34

> *"But seek ye first the kingdom of God, and his righteousness; and all these things will be added unto you. Take therefore no thought for the morrow: for the morrow shall take thought for the things of itself. Sufficient unto the day is the evil thereof."*

God is telling us to never worry. You could say it's a New Covenant commandment. Just don't go there! If you feel yourself drifting into worry, "Nip it in the bud!" Shift your mind to the word, begin to think on good things. Philippians tells us how we are to think.

Philippians 4:8

> *"Finally, brethren, whatsoever things are true, whatsoever things are honest, whatsoever things are just, whatsoever*

things are pure, whatsoever things are lovely, whatsoever things are of good report; if there be any virtue, and if there be any praise, think on these things."

I'm not saying it's always easy to think good thoughts when all Hades seems to be breaking loose, but it is something we must exercise and learn to do.

The Christian life is likened to a tree or plant that begins with a seed and grows to produce fruit. What does it take to grow a plant? It takes seed, soil, water, sunshine, nutrients and sometimes a little fertilizer. Another word for fertilizer is (And I'll be nice and say) manure. Sometimes we have to go through a lot of manure. I mean like the t-shirt says sometimes manure just happens! But manure is often necessary for us to grow, so we need to learn to not allow the hardships of what we are going through to make us bitter but better, to allow them to work growth and fruit in our lives to the glory of God.

CHAPTER 16

TRANSFORMED BY THE WORD

Once again we see the vital importance of meditating on the word of God. Romans 12:2 says that we are not to be conformed to this world or poured into this world's mold but instead we are to be transformed by the renewing of our minds.

An apple tree branch does not have to strive or struggle to produce apples. It naturally produces apples as it abides in the tree. And as we abide in the word the fruit that is inside will come out. We will bear fruit as we abide in God's word.

Now Romans 12:1 says that we are to present ourselves a living sacrifice to the Lord. How do we present ourselves as a living sacrifice to the Lord? By not conforming to the world and the way the world thinks. By not being poured into the mold of this world and by renewing our minds. The Bible says that we are transformed by the renewing of our minds.

Transformed means metamorphism, which is the same word used when a caterpillar turns into a butterfly. As our minds are renewed to the truth of God's word we will literally be transformed from the inside out by the power of God.

The way we think is the most dominant force in our lives. Proverbs 23:7 "as a man thinks in his heart so is he."

We need to be re-programming our minds and allow the word to change our thinking. Many of us have had wrong thinking that has come from the influence of this world. Many in the church today have had wrong religious teaching that has influenced their thinking and needs to be reprogrammed to the truth of the New Covenant and the Gospel of grace.

The word for renewing is actually the word renovation. When somebody renovates a house they usually go in and take the old materials out and install brand-new materials. We need to allow the Holy Spirit to be our spiritual carpenter and change our old ways of thinking. That is to take out our old thoughts and replace those old thoughts with His thoughts according to the word of God. This sounds like a familiar scripture doesn't it? Look at Isaiah 55:7-13

> *"Let the wicked forsake his way, and the unrighteous man his thoughts: and let him return unto the Lord, and he will*

have mercy upon him; and to our God, for he will abundantly pardon. For my thoughts are not your thoughts, neither are your ways my ways, saith the Lord. For as the heavens are higher than the earth, so are my ways higher than your ways, and my thoughts than your thoughts. For as the rain cometh down, and the snow from heaven, and returns not thither, but waters the earth, and makes it bring forth and bud, that it may give seed to the sower, and bread to the eater: So shall my word be that goeth forth out of my mouth: it shall not return unto me void, but it shall accomplish that which I please, and it shall prosper in the thing whereto I sent it. For ye shall go out with joy, and be led forth with peace: the mountains and the hills shall break forth before you into singing, and all the trees of the field shall clap their hands. Instead of the thorn shall come up the fir tree, and instead of the brier shall come up the myrtle tree: and it shall be to the Lord for a name, for an everlasting sign that shall not be cut off."

Wow! What a promise by the Lord for all who will forsake their own thoughts and ways and seek only the thoughts and ways of the Lord! As we do this our minds will be renewed to the truth of God's word and we will go forth and see an abundant harvest go before us.

We cannot lose by renewing our minds to the word of God. As we renew our minds, God promises to bless us. We often limit God by our limited humanistic thinking. As we meditate on God's word, exchanging our thoughts for His thoughts, it will cause the faith that He has already placed inside of us to explode.

CHAPTER 17

WHY TESTS?

Tests are absolutely essential for God's power to rest and to be displayed in and through us. One of the main reasons God put the tree of the knowledge of good and evil in the garden was to give man a choice. The freedom to choose God's word over all fleshly desire is necessary in order for God's power to be displayed in and through us. As we continue to make the right choices, choosing God's word and God's way over our own desire, we will continue to display the strength and power of God in and through our lives.

Now, as I began to meditate on this, I was reminded about Jesus and how He began His earthly ministry. First we know that when Jesus was baptized in water He heard these words: "This is my beloved Son in whom I am well pleased".

Matthew 3:16-17
"And Jesus, when he was baptized, went

> *up straightway out of the water: and, lo, the heavens were opened unto him, and he saw the Spirit of God descending like a dove, and lighting upon him: And lo a voice from heaven, saying, This is my beloved Son, in whom I am well pleased."*

Let me say this, before we as Christians can ever become effective in ministry we must also hear these words, "This is my beloved son in whom I am well pleased." We need to firmly understand and believe that through the new birth, and because we have been put into Christ, we are now very pleasing in the eyes of God. There is no more sin or separation between us and God. Unless we understand this truth we cannot be effective in ministry to others. If we sense that we do not measure up to God we will always feel a sense of separation and condemnation which in turn only keeps us engaged to self ministry. Those in condemnation are engaged in full-time ministry to themselves. So we must embrace these same words that Jesus heard and embraced: "This is my beloved son in whom I am well pleased." Now, right after Jesus heard these words, something else took place.

Luke 4:1-4
> *"And Jesus being full of the Holy Ghost returned from Jordan, and was led by the Spirit into the wilderness, Being forty days tempted of the devil. And in those*

WHY TESTS?

> *days he did eat nothing: and when they were ended, he afterward hungered. And the devil said unto him, If thou be the Son of God, command this stone that it be made bread. And Jesus answered him, saying, It is written, That man shall not live by bread alone, but by every word of God."*

Right after Jesus was baptized; He was led by the Holy Spirit into the wilderness to be tested by the devil. In the past I never could really understand why the Holy Spirit would lead Jesus into the wilderness to be tempted by the devil until I saw what took place after the wilderness temptation.

Luke 4:13-14

> *"And when the devil had ended all the temptation, he departed from him for a season. And Jesus returned in the power of the Spirit into Galilee: and there went out a fame of him through all the region round about."*

Notice that Jesus was led into the wilderness by the Holy Spirit, but after He had successfully overcome every temptation that the devil had thrown at Him, Jesus then returned in the power of the Spirit. The wilderness temptation was necessary for Jesus to walk in the power of the Spirit and to begin His earthly ministry.

I'M SAVED! NOW WHAT?

Paul received the revelation of God's strength and power being perfected through him as he faced a constant barrage of harassment and persecution from many of the Pharisees who continually followed Paul around, doing their best to discredit his apostleship and message. The term "messenger of satan" is in reference to those that Satan raised up to discredit the true messengers and gospel of Christ.

2 Corinthians 12:7-10 (AMP)
> *"And to keep me from being puffed up and too much elated by the exceeding greatness (preeminence) of these revelations, there was given me a thorn ([a]a splinter) in the flesh, a messenger of Satan, to rack and buffet and harass me, to keep me from being excessively exalted. Three times I called upon the Lord and besought [Him] about this and begged that it might depart from me; But He said to me, My grace (My favor and loving-kindness and mercy) is enough for you [sufficient against any danger and enables you to bear the trouble manfully]; for My strength and power are made perfect (fulfilled and completed) and [b]show themselves most effective in [your] weakness. Therefore, I will all the more gladly glory in my weaknesses and infirmities, that the strength and power of Christ (the Messiah) may rest (yes, may*

WHY TESTS?

> *[c]pitch a tent over and dwell) upon me! So for the sake of Christ, I am well pleased and take pleasure in infirmities, insults, hardships, persecutions, perplexities and distresses; for when I am weak [[d]in human strength], then am I [truly] strong (able, powerful [e]in divine strength)."*

Again, Jesus Himself was led into the wilderness by the Holy Spirit to be tempted by the devil, and because He made the right choice which was always according to God's word over the flesh, the power of God and the glory of God were then released through Him.

Now, If Jesus was tempted, how much more will we not be tried and tempted? But I believe the key to overcoming trials is to understand the reason behind the trials.

1 Peter 4:12-

> *"Beloved, think it not strange concerning the fiery trial which is to try you, as though some strange thing happened unto you: But rejoice, inasmuch as ye are partakers of Christ's sufferings; that, when his glory shall be revealed, ye may be glad also with exceeding joy. If ye be reproached for the name of Christ, happy are ye; for the spirit of glory and of God*

> *rests upon you: on their part he is evil spoken of, but on your part he is glorified."*

We shouldn't think it strange when trials come our way, especially in the form of persecution. In fact, if we are walking according to the truth of the gospel, we are guaranteed resistance and opposition.

2 Timothy 3:12
> *"All that will live godly in Christ Jesus shall suffer persecution."*

Galatians 5:11
> *"And I, brethren, if I yet preach circumcision, why do I yet suffer persecution? Then is the offense of the cross ceased."*

If we are proclaiming the true gospel, we will suffer persecution. And why? Because the devil hates the true gospel. The true gospel releases the power of God for salvation to everyone who believes. We need to understand that all trials and temptations will only make us stronger and freer in Christ as we respond to them according to God's Word.

Remember the three Hebrew children who were tossed into the fire? As they responded in the right way to God's Word, the only thing that was burned was the ropes that bound them.

WHY TESTS?

Did you know that with God we never fail any test? We just keep getting to take them over and over again until we pass.

James 1:2-4

> *"Consider it wholly joyful, my brethren, whenever you are enveloped in or encounter trials of any sort or fall into various temptations. Be assured and understand that the trial and proving of your faith bring out endurance and steadfastness and patience. But let endurance and steadfastness and patience have full play and do a thorough work, so that you may be [people] perfectly and fully developed [with no defects], lacking in nothing.*

> We have been given the measure of faith to believe just like Jesus believed.

CHAPTER 18

FAITH IS THE BRIDGE

Faith is the bridge between the natural and the supernatural world. Faith appropriates and makes manifest what already exist in the unseen or the spirit world.

For example, in the spirit realm we are already healed. Faith brings the healing that we already have and manifests it into the physical realm. Peter said to the lame man, "Silver and gold have I none but such as I have I give to you." What did Peter have? He had healing. Peter believed what he already had and by faith brought it out from the spirit realm, gave it to the lame man in the physical realm and the lame man was healed.

This is what Jesus did when He fed the five thousand with five loaves and two fish. The provision was already there to feed the five thousand in the unseen realm and Jesus, by faith, took what already existed in the unseen realm and it was made manifest into the physical seen realm.

I'M SAVED! NOW WHAT?

Hebrews 11:3
> *"Through faith we understand that the worlds were framed by the word of God, so that things which are seen were not made of things which do appear."*

All we see today was created or came out from the unseen spiritual world. Are we living more by what we see or by what we don't see? It does not take the God kind of faith to believe what you can see but it does take the God kind of faith to believe what you cannot see. What did Jesus say about those who exercise this kind of faith?

John 20:29
> *"Jesus saith unto him, Thomas, because thou hast seen me, thou hast believed: blessed are they that have not seen, and yet have believed."*

Did you know that we as Christians today actually have more faith than any of the prophets of old ever had and more than any of the disciples before the cross ever had? We have been given the measure of faith to believe just like Jesus believed. We have the same faith that Jesus had to operate in the unseen world and to see what is in the unseen world manifest into the seen world.

Also, did you know that we who are in the New Covenant have something far greater than any prophet that ever existed in the Old Covenant? This includes Abraham, Isaac, Jacob Moses, Elijah and all the rest. "What, little ole me greater then Abraham, Moses, Elijah, David and all the great men of faith in the Old Testament?" Yep! And before you call me a heretic read your Bible.

Matthew 11:11
> *"Verily I say unto you, Among them that are born of women there hath not risen a greater than John the Baptist: notwithstanding he that is least in the kingdom of heaven is greater than he."*

What does it say? The least in the kingdom of God today is greater than any prophet that has ever existed including John the Baptist. You might say, "How can that be?" Because of the One Who now lives in you! Greater is He that's in you then he that's in the world.

None of the great prophets of old had in them what you have now in you today! I'm sure they are looking down from heaven and thinking why don't they see what is in them? They have the entire Trinity in them. They have the Father, Son and Holy Ghost in them and they don't even know it! They have the kingdom of God in them and they don't even know it!" They are saying, "We had God with us but they have God in them! We had natural faith but they have the very supernatural faith of God in them!"

Do you believe that God lives in you and wants to manifest Himself through you? Do you believe that you have Christ in you and the faith of Christ in you? We already have been given all the blessings of God in heavenly places in Christ in us.

Ephesians 1:3
> *"Blessed be the God and Father of our Lord Jesus Christ, who hath blessed us with all spiritual blessings in heavenly places in Christ:"*

We are surrounded by a great cloud of witnesses which include all the great prophets of old and they are rooting us on and praying that we will wake up to all we already have in Christ.

Hebrews 12:1-2
> *"Wherefore seeing we also are compassed about with so great a cloud of witnesses, let us lay aside every weight, and the sin which doth so easily beset us, and let us run with patience the race that is set before us, Looking unto Jesus the author and finisher of our faith;"*

We need to meditate on the Scriptures concerning these things, because they are true.

CHAPTER 19

HOW TO RELEASE FAITH

Philemon 1:6
"That the communication of thy faith may become effectual by the acknowledging of every good thing which is in you in Christ Jesus."

Our faith becomes effectual as we acknowledge every good thing that has already been put in us in Christ. I encourage every believer to meditate on the promises of God that He has already lavished on us in Christ.

2 Peter 1:4

"Whereby are given unto us exceeding great and precious promises: that by these ye might be partakers of the divine nature, having escaped the corruption that is in the world through lust."

I'M SAVED! NOW WHAT?

As we meditate on the things already given to us by God in Christ and agree and believe these things are true for us, we begin to experience from the inside out His divine nature and part of that divine nature is the faith of Christ. The other part of this is to not only believe that these promises are ours but to also confess them or speak them.

Romans 10:8-10

> *"But what saith it? The word is nigh thee, even in thy mouth, and in thy heart: that is, the word of faith, which we preach; That if thou shalt confess with thy mouth the Lord Jesus, and shalt believe in thine heart that God hath raised him from the dead, thou shalt be saved. For with the heart man believes unto righteousness; and with the mouth confession is made unto salvation."*

Notice Paul said he had the word of faith in his heart and in his mouth. This means he knew that Christ was in him, the faith of Christ was in him and all that he had to do is open up his mouth and preach to let it all come out.

Also in verse 10 it says that man believes in his heart unto righteousness, but with his mouth man speaks unto salvation. We already know that the Greek word for salvation is *sozo* which means healing, deliverance, and a host of all that we have been given

HOW TO RELEASE FAITH

in Christ. Speaking is a huge part of appropriating the faith we have.

Matthew 21:21
> *"Jesus answered and said unto them, Verily I say unto you, If ye have faith, and doubt not, ye shall not only do this which is done to the fig tree, but also if ye shall say unto this mountain, Be thou removed, and be thou cast into the sea; it shall be done."*

Jesus said if we have faith and doubt not, we can speak to fig trees and the mountain and there will be a response. Well, first of all we already know that we have faith because the Bible says that as Christians have all been given the measure of faith of Christ. We have the same faith Christ had in Him, but the other part of this Scripture is that we doubt not! One of the only things that can stop the faith of Christ from operating in and through our lives is doubt or unbelief.

How do we deal with unbelief? We deal with it by meditating on the truth of God's word. God's word is called the sword of the Spirit that can cut away all unbelief in and out of our lives.

The word will also stir up the faith in us. There are only two things that ever stopped the faith of Christ from working, ignorance and unbelief. And these are the only things that stop the church from releasing the faith of Christ.

I'M SAVED! NOW WHAT?

As we meditate on who we are and what we have in Christ and begin to believe and confess these things, it will begin to release what God has put inside. Faith is released through confession

CHAPTER 20

WATER WALKERS

Calling all Water Walkers!

How do we become water walkers, or how can we begin to walk in the supernatural power of God?

Matthew 14:25-29

> *"And in the fourth watch of the night Jesus went unto them, walking on the sea. And when the disciples saw him walking on the sea, they were troubled, saying, It is a spirit; and they cried out for fear. But straightway Jesus spake unto them, saying, Be of good cheer; it is I; be not afraid. And Peter answered him and said, Lord, if it be thou, bid me come unto thee on the water. And he said, Come. And when Peter was come down*

out of the ship, he walked on the water, to go to Jesus."

First, to be water walkers like Peter, we must be willing to step out of our boats and take some risks. We cannot allow fear of the unknown to keep us in the security of our boats. We must choose to move out of our comfort zones and learn to trust God. Many times God will speak to us and lead us to do things that are far bigger than we could ever comprehend doing, or even have the physical or financial ability to do. This is where real trust comes in. The question is, "Are we willing to do whatever it is that God asks us to do even if it makes no sense, or are we going to analyze out every move before we take that step of faith that God has shown us to take?"

We know walking on water or even feeding five thousand people with five loaves and two fish or turning water into wine is not scientifically reasonable, but with God all things are possible. We, in our own natural ability, could never do these things. I know of people who have actually tried to walk on water and they always go right to the bottom! So, what I'm not saying is, we just try in our own ability to do these things. What I am saying is that we need to be willing to do whatever God shows us or calls us to do without hesitation. Even if it does not add up or make sense. If we will learn to stay out of our peanut-brain logic and simply respond to God with child-like faith, we will begin to see God move through our lives in a supernatural way.

In order to become water walkers, we must also learn to become doers of the word and not hearers only. That is, we need to put feet to our faith. The faith we have been given when we received Christ will never work if there is no corresponding action behind it. I believe the book of James is one of the most misunderstood books in the Bible. When James was speaking about faith being dead without works, he was not implying that we are saved by works. I believe what he was really telling us was that faith will not work unless there is some kind of corresponding action behind it.

For example, if Peter would not have put his foot over the boat and taken the action to walk on water, he would never have walked on the water. I mean Peter could have believed all day long that he could walk on water but until he actually put feet to his faith, his faith was dead.

Hearing God means to not only know what the written word says, but it also means to have an ear to hear what the Spirit is showing us to do. We, as New Covenant believers, are called to be led by the promptings of the Holy Spirit. This is how Jesus walked, and this is how we are called to walk as well. (Romans 7:6)

When Jesus told Peter to come to Him, Peter got out of the boat and walked on the word of God. Peter's focus was not on the water, which really represented the beyond all logic and impossible thing to do, but Peter's focus was on Jesus and His word.

I'M SAVED! NOW WHAT?

Listen, God's word will always hold us up, but it's also vital to keep our eyes on Jesus and God's word to stay up! Remember, Peter began to sink when he turned his eyes off of Jesus and back to his own senses. We need to understand that Jesus is our confidence, Jesus is grace, Jesus is the One we are to always look and listen to. Without Christ we can do nothing, but with Him there is nothing we can't do! Even the impossible!

Now, let me say that as soon as we step out of the boat, there will also come some things to distract you. Often times it will be the voice of doubt and unbelief that will come to you and say, "What are you doing? You can't do that! It's impossible!" These voices are voices of carnal logic and judgment that operate in the seen realm or the five senses. The voice of carnality will always make every effort to get you out of faith and into unbelief. And unbelief's mission is to keep you from stepping out of the boat, or if you do step out of the boat, to get you to sink or tempt you to jump back into the boat that you just stepped out of!

It's amazing that Jesus came walking on water more than once to demonstrate to the disciples that the supernatural power of God is really no big deal for God. I mean He created it all and He holds it all in the palm of His hand.

The Bible records another instance where Jesus came walking out to the disciples on water during a fierce storm and Jesus was walking like He was on a casual stroll along the beach. How could He do this?

He could do it because His attention was fully on the Father and what the Father was showing Him to do. Didn't Jesus tell us that all things were possible for those who would trust God?

Now, we know again that Peter began to sink when He got his eyes off Jesus and on to the storm. What we need to understand is that it wasn't the storm that caused Peter to sink. It was the fact that Peter took his eyes off Jesus and God's Word. It could have been a sunny day with no wind and Peter would have still sunk, because he took his eyes off of Jesus. The storm had little to do with it.

If we want to become water walkers, we have to keep our eyes fixed on Jesus and become not only hearers of His Word but radical doers. Faith comes by hearing and hearing by the Word. In order for faith to work it will take action, and often times that action will require us to step out of our own logic and trust God.

One thing that the Lord just drew my attention to was that first of all Peter was not a perfect person. A lot of people have disqualified themselves from walking in the supernatural power of God because they see themselves as imperfect people that are way to full of flaws, and therefore are not qualified to do supernatural things like the Apostles did. Listen, we need to understand that when the Apostles did all of these supernatural miracles not one of them was perfect. They all had flaws! Peter had a lot of flaws, James and John had a lot of flaws! None of them were by the flesh perfect. We need to understand that God uses imperfect people to do supernatural things. None of us by the flesh are perfect. Now, let me say that if you are born again, in your spirit you are righteous and perfect, but in your mortal flesh we still all fall short. We are to never allow our fleshly imperfections to ever disqualify us from walking in the supernatural power of God.

Today, many have also allowed their traditions, or the doctrines of men, to convince them that God no longer uses people today to demonstrate the supernatural power of God. Many denominations actually teach that the power of God passed away with the Apostles! Where they got this idea from I don't know, but this idea is really not from God. I believe it is a doctrine of devils to teach that God no longer desires to supernaturally work through believers to heal the sick or deliver people from demonic influences. The devil loves it when God's people no longer believe in the supernatural power of God, because it leaves them powerless and carnal. But this is not how God says His kingdom is to function or to be advanced. Let's see what the Bible has to say about the kingdom of God and the power of God.

I Corinthians 4:20
"For the kingdom of God is not in word, but in power."

1 Corinthians 2:13
> *"And my speech and my preaching was not with enticing words of man's wisdom, but in demonstration of the Spirit and of power, that your faith should not stand in the wisdom of men, but in the power of God."*

It is clear that God still desires to demonstrate His power through the church, but again we have often allowed the doctrines of men to disqualify us from walking in the supernatural power of God.

We have also allowed our own imperfections to disqualify us from walking in the supernatural power of God. We see ourselves as not perfect enough to be used by God in a supernatural way. "If God will use anyone, it will be the preacher or the evangelist, but I'm just a poor ole struggling church member, God could never use me like that." Let me say this, one of the main reasons that we see ourselves as poor old struggling church members full of imperfections is because we still do not understand what grace has already accomplished for us and Who lives in us, that is, in our spirit.

What we need to understand is, when we said yes to Jesus and were born again, we were also created righteous. In other words, as born again believers we are not just forgiven, we are righteous and perfect because we have been baptized into Jesus, Who is righteous and perfect! So that all that Jesus is, we have become! Galatians 2:20 says it's no longer I that live, but Christ Who now lives in me.

2 Corinthians 5:17 says:
> *"Therefore if any man be in Christ, he is a new creature: old things are passed away; behold, all things are become new."*

The Bible says that when we received Christ all the old things passed away and all has become new and all things are now of God. It also says that we have the same Spirit living in us that raised Christ from the dead!

Today we are as qualified to walk in the supernatural power of God as Jesus is. We should never disqualify ourselves from walking in the supernatural power of God. Jesus gave the disciples this commission before He was taken into heaven:

Mark 6:15-18
> *"And he said unto them, Go ye into all the world, and preach the gospel to every creature. He that believes and is baptized shall be saved; but he that believes not shall be damned. And these signs shall follow them that believe; In my name shall they cast out devils; they shall speak with new tongues; They shall take up serpents; and if they drink any deadly thing, it shall not hurt them; they shall lay hands on the sick, and they shall recover."*

WATER WALKERS

Peter did not walk on water because he was perfect. He walked on water because Jesus said he could and Peter simply believed it. The supernatural will follow those who believe. For those who do not believe, they will not have to worry about the supernatural following them.

The Lord also drew my attention to another reason why Peter walked on water. His impulsive personality tended to get him into a lot of trouble at times, like the time he cut someone's ear off in the garden! But Peter's impulsiveness also caused him to simply jump out of the boat and recklessly obey God's word.

I believe, like Peter, we also need to be quicker to just step out and do whatever God shows or tells us to do and not over-analyze things. We need to do whatever God says whether it makes sense or not! Instant obedience will always cripple second guessing!

Remember when they ran out of wine at the wedding that Jesus attended? This was actually one of the first recorded miracles that Jesus performed. Jesus told the servants to fill the pots with water and serve it to the guests. This made no sense at all. But Mary, the mother of Jesus, told the servants that whatever He says, just do it! I believ we will begin to see more miracles happen as we just do whatever God tells us to do, and stop over-analyzing things. Peter would have never walked on water if he would have looked at the water and said, "That it's not scientifically possible to walk on water, it makes no sense." Listen, I believe that today God is trying to move us beyond our own logic and reason and what makes sense into supernatural faith.

Listen, the God-kind of faith, most of the time, is not logical - it doesn't compute! God wants us to begin to live more by what we can't see than what we can see. He wants to move us from the carnal (seen) realm to the supernatural (unseen) realm.

The world says, "I will believe it when I see it!" But Jesus said, "You will see it when you step out and believe."

As I read the biblical account about Peter walking on water, I believe the Lord began to show me that when Jesus beckoned Peter to come to Him and Peter, with corresponding action stepped out of the boat, he really didn't step out on water, he stepped out on the word of God. God's word is what really held Peter up, and God's word will always hold us up as well. As we begin to hear God's word and radically step out of our boats to do whatever God says, even if it's beyond our own logic, we will begin to see more of the supernatural power of God manifest through our lives. Today I believe God is looking for more water walkers.

CHAPTER 21

THE SUPERNATURAL BECOMING NATURAL

The other day, as I was waking up, I felt the Lord say, "As we begin to expect and see healing and miracles as no big deal and common, we will see more healing and miracles happen." The one reason we don't see more miracles is due to the fact that we don't expect miracles and healing. We look at the supernatural as a rare, uncommon thing and we really do not even anticipate or expect them to happen. We often see miracles as climbing Mt. Everest or way too difficult and impossible for us to do, and only a few will ever do this. Miracles should be seen more as a speed bump than climbing Mt. Everest - it's no big deal!

As we begin to see miracles as no big deal for God and begin to anticipate miracles, we will see more miracles. Signs and wonders should not be a rare occurrence but a common occurrence for the Spirit-led believer.

Jesus told us these signs would follow all those who believe. He said that they would lay hands on the sick and they would recover. But notice, it says these signs would follow them that believe; if you don't believe in signs and wonders then you don't have to worry about seeing them because signs only follow those who believe.

We should never look at miracles as uncommon impossibilities but instead, we should look at them as common to us, just a simple part of the ministry that God has called us to do. Jesus said if anyone says to this mountain be plucked up and cast into the sea then it will be done. In other words, Jesus was teaching us how to approach the seemingly huge impossibilities for man, as they are very easy and very possible with God.

We need to take more of a casual approach to healing and laying hands on the sick than seeing it as an impossible task! Listen, God told us to lay hands on the sick and believe. It's not our job to heal; it's our job to believe healing is still available today and to lay hands on the sick.

Faith never makes any sense. This is why God has instructed us to live by faith! God wants to get us beyond our own reasoning and carnality and into supernatural living. Faith is the only way to live a supernatural, Spirit-led life.

This is why God has instructed His people to do so many things that in the natural made absolutely no sense! God gets us beyond reason and into faith. Faith is where the supernatural flows and works. Faith is where miracles take place.

Remember the first miracle of Jesus, turning the water into wine? He told the servants to do something that absolutely made no sense at all. He told them to take water and fill the wine vessels with water and to serve it to the wedding guests. Can you imagine what went through the servants' minds? They were probably thinking, "This is crazy! This makes no sense at all." In other words, this is beyond reason. But Mary, the mother of Jesus, told the servants, "Whatever He says just do it." And the servants simply went and did what was beyond reason and obeyed the Lord and His word, and then the miracle took place.

Signs and wonders will also begin to follow our lives as soon as we simply take God at His word and move out and begin to do what He says beyond reason.

The Bible says that we, who are the just, are to live by faith and not by sight. Christians who are living by their own natural five senses are called carnal Christians. We have got to move beyond Christian humanism and begin to walk by faith and by the Spirit of the living God, Who now lives in us; this is true Christianity.

Now as you lay hands on the sick and pray, visualize your hand as being the hand of Jesus. Why? Because we are really just an extension in this physical realm of the power of God! The Bible says that same power that raised Christ from the dead lives in you!

Romans 8:11
> *"But if the Spirit of him that raised up Jesus from the dead dwell in you, he that raised up Christ from the dead shall also quicken your mortal bodies by his Spirit that lives in you."*

This is what it means to heal others in Jesus' name. Because you are in Jesus, then the same works that He did, you can do also, because you are the very vessel or container of God.

Now we must put feet to our faith to see faith work. In other words, we must put action to faith to see miracles happen. This is why we speak the word and anoint with oil and we lay hands on people - this is the action part. This is why we speak to the mountain to be removed! We speak directly to the illness and command it to go!

This is the action part of faith. Remember, Jesus always put action to His faith. One time He told someone to take up their bed and walk; another time He said wash yourself in the pool; another time He said go show yourselves to the priest. One time a woman with an issue of blood pushed her way through the crowd to get her healing. In other words, there is always a corresponding action for faith to work. When a preacher tells someone to run around after praying

THE SUPERNATURAL BECOMING NATURAL

for them or move their arms or legs, this is the corresponding action part.

The book of James has often been misunderstood as saying that James was telling us that we are saved by works or good deeds and not by faith, which seems contrary to what the Apostle Paul said in Ephesians 2:8-9:

> *"For by grace are ye saved through faith; and that not of yourselves: it is the gift of God: Not of works, lest any man should boast."*

What I have come to realize is what James was really showing us was how faith really does work. Faith works when we put action to it. In other words, your car will not go anywhere if you don't get in the car and turn the key. If we want to see the supernatural power of God flow through our lives, we must get in the driver's seat and turn the key on!

We can say we believe in healing, but are we laying hands on the sick and commanding sickness to leave? Or have we adopted a kind of "Que sera, sera", whatever will be, will be attitude? Saying, "Well if God wants to heal people then He will heal them with or without me". But God wants to use you to heal people. We are the containers of God. We are the vehicles that God wants to use to demonstrate His power through!

I'M SAVED! NOW WHAT?

Remember the five loaves two fish that Jesus used to feed five thousand? How did this happen? He took what He had and made them sit down and began to give out what He had. This was faith in action!

In another case, Jesus only took four loaves and fed seven thousand. In other words, the bigger the need, the bigger the miracle. In God's economy, the bigger the problem the simpler and easier it is - it's no problem, no big deal for God.

We should never look at the need and say, "Oh, this will take little faith, while other needs will take more faith". No, if you have faith the size of a mustard seed then you can move any mountain. The Bible says that we have already been given the measure of the faith of Christ! In other words, we have the same faith of Christ that Christ had when he walked this earth! That's amazing!

Romans 12:3
> "For I say, through the grace given unto me, to every man that is among you, not to think of himself more highly than he ought to think; but to think soberly, according as God hath dealt to every man the measure of faith."

Notice that it does not say that to each is given a different measure of faith but the measure of faith. In other words, we all have the same big scoop of faith. I used to think that this was saying that some had a pinch of faith and others a bigger pinch of faith, like the big faith such as R.W. Schambach had; a real big scoop of faith. But what I have come to realize is that we have all been given the same measure of faith.

Cancer is no big deal to the resurrection power of Christ! We can command cancer to go. We can speak to that mountain of cancer to leave and it has to obey. Now Isaiah 53:1 asks whose report will we believe?

> *"Who hath believed our report? And to whom is the arm of the Lord revealed?"*

The arm of The Lord will be revealed to those who believe His report. When the doctor comes in and gives you his report will you automatically believe it or will you turn to believe the report of the Lord that says by the stripes of Christ you have been healed?

I realize that it makes more sense in the natural realm to believe the doctor's report, but in the faith realm or in the unseen realm we are called to believe the report of the Lord. This is how faith works. I believe God wants to move us beyond our own five natural senses and into the supernatural realm, where we begin to believe it before we see it and as we do, we will see the miraculous.

We need to begin to see miracles as a common occurrence for us - as no big deal. Miracles for the believer should be just another extension of who we are and what we have been called to do. Did you know that raising of the dead is a fundamental foundational teaching for the believer?

Now remember when the disciples were in a storm struggling and rowing and toiling and all of a sudden they saw Jesus walking out on the water, like He was taking a casual stroll along the beach? It's like Jesus was telling them, "This ain't no big deal"... I mean Jesus almost walked right by them until they cried out, "Save us!" I really do believe that one of the great lessons that Jesus was showing them was that it doesn't matter how extreme the circumstances are, or how big the mountain seems to be; it is still no big deal or no match for God.

So why are we to see mountains as no big deal? I believe God is telling us that we have to get beyond all our natural intellectual reasoning and simply believe God. We serve a big God and nothing is too difficult for Him!

I was just reminded by the Lord of what kept God's people out of the promised land. They said the people are like giants and we are like grasshoppers. In other words, they saw the problem as a much bigger deal than their God! Are we seeing our circumstances as bigger than God? Of course, this is not how Joshua and Caleb saw it. They said, "it ain't no big deal, we are well able to take the land!" Why? Because God is with us and He is bigger than anything we will ever face.

Remember when all of Israel was intimidated by one giant called Goliath? They cowered back in fear, and then here comes a little shepherd boy with eyes of faith that said, "Who is this uncircumcised Philistine that he should defy the armies of the living God!" And with five smooth stones, which really is a symbol of God's grace, he easily brought the giant down and cut his head off. To David, this giant was no big deal compared to God.

Now when someone comes to us for healing, don't allow your intellect to kick in and think, "Wow, this is a great sickness, I hope it works when I pray, what if it doesn't?" Stay out of your reasoning and stick with the word!

Healing someone is not a matter of yelling, screaming, shaking it into someone, sweating, and jumping up and down. It's a matter of God's grace. Healings and miracles are simply a part of the gospel of grace. Psalm 103 says He forgives all our sins and heals all our diseases. Healing is part of the benefit package of grace.

We need to treat healing as the easiest thing to do. It's not about begging, pleading, working up a sweat or a lather. It's about simply believing what God has provided and speaking it. Jesus said, "Which is more difficult: to tell someone their sins are forgiven, or rise and be healed?" We are to look at forgiveness of sins and healing as one in the same. They come as a package deal in the word.

Matthew 8:16-17

> *"When the even was come, they brought unto him many that were possessed with devils: and he cast out the spirits with his*

I'M SAVED! NOW WHAT?

word, and healed all that were sick: That it might be fulfilled which was spoken by Esaias the prophet, saying, Himself took our infirmities, and bare our sicknesses."

Again, this was a quote from Isaiah 53 that says, "Who has believed our report and to whom is the arm of The Lord revealed?" God is waiting for somebody to believe His report. This again goes back to who's waiting on who? Are we waiting on God to heal or is God waiting on us to believe that He already has healed us?

God wants the supernatural to become natural in the believer's life, and I believe that. This is the year when the supernatural will become more natural for the believer.

One of the main reasons that we do not see more of the power of God working in the church is due to the fact that we have mixed the old and the new, or law and grace, together. The law came by Moses, but grace and truth through Jesus. When we mix law with grace together, we will frustrate grace, and grace is the power of God. In fact Jesus Himself is grace. That's again why the Bible says when we fall back to the law then Christ becomes of no effect! Christ, and His power, will cease to work in a church bound by the law and carnality! Before we can see demonstration, we must have a revelation of the grace of God. We are no longer under the law but grace.

We need to kick Ishmael and his mama out of the house before the power of God can be fully released in and through our lives. Ishmael represents the works of the flesh, carnality, and law. We must also change our garments or our dirty clothes!

Zachariah 3:3-4 says we must change the filthy garments .. And put on the new. This is echoed in the New Covenant ... put off the old and put on the new you created in righteousness.

These dirty clothes do not represent sin as religion has often taught, but they actually represent self righteousness.

If we are to see God's power demonstrated in the church, we must put off our own self righteous acts and put on the righteousness of God that comes through faith in the finished work of Christ. Zachariah 4:6 states that we also need to realize that it is not by our might or power but by His Spirit that we are to walk and live. This is the New Covenant way! We are not to be led by the letter of the law or flesh but by faith and the prompting of the Spirit. (Romans 7:6)

Zachariah 4: 7 also speaks of grace. Grace is how we are to live and do all ministry. We are to speak grace. Grace to the mountain. Grace releases the power of Christ in us to move every mountain. Not law, not flesh, but grace. Those who say we are over preaching grace simply do not have a revelation of the New Covenant. It is a covenant of grace and truth.

Again, grace and law cannot be mixed. Law frustrates grace. One of the main reasons that we are

I'M SAVED! NOW WHAT?

not seeing more mountains removed and more miracles happen is because we have mixed law and grace together.

CHAPTER 22

THE TRUE NATURE OF GOD

2 Corinthians 10:4-5 (Amp) *"For the weapons of our warfare are not physical [weapons of flesh and blood], but they are mighty before God for the overthrow and destruction of strongholds, [Inasmuch as we] refute arguments and theories and reasonings and every proud and lofty thing that sets itself up against the [true] knowledge of God; and we lead every thought and purpose away captive into the obedience of Christ (the Messiah, the Anointed One),"*

We need to understand that today we have a real unseen enemy. He is called the god of this world, Satan, the devil, the deceiver and accuser. He has, since the very beginning of creation, had one goal in mind: to lie, deceive, and to keep people that God has created, blind from knowing the truth.

Now many might say the truth about what? The truth about Who God really is – the true nature of God and God's real intention for us.
One of Satan's main missions is to distort our view of God and cause us to question God's integrity, character, and intentions toward us.

In the Scripture above, we see that God has provided us with weapons to refute arguments, reasonings, and theories that set themselves up against the true knowledge of God.

Again, one of the main things that Satan wants to do is to keep us from the true knowledge of God. Many in the world today have reasons why they do not live for God. Most of these reasons are based on lies they have believed from the accuser. Satan has blinded their minds from the truth.

2 Corinthians 4:4
> *"The God of this world has put blinders on most people in this world to keep them busy and distracted from knowing the real truth of God's great love for them."*

Many today have a wrong view of Who God is, and much of this view comes from religion. Religion has painted a wrong view of God. Many have characterized God as a very unstable, emotional being, that can be in a great mood one minute and then the next minute wiping a whole bunch of people

THE TRUE NATURE OF GOD

out because He doesn't like what they're doing.

God gets almost no credit for the good things that happen. Howver, He always gets the blame when bad things happen. For example, if something really good happens, a lot of people give the credit to luck or good fortune. They will say things like, "Yes, I was lucky!" But if something bad happens, they blame God. They will say things like, "God, why did you bring this misfortune to me? "

Even the insurance companies blame God for all natural disasters, calling them "Acts of God!" Why not call them acts of Satan or the devil? The devil's job is to make people believe that God is a harsh, cruel, almost psychotic God that loves to see people in pain and can't wait to throw many of them into hell! But when I first came to know God it was through this scripture.

John 3:16-17 (AMP)
> *"For God so greatly loved and dearly prized the world that He [even] gave up His only begotten (unique) Son, so that whoever believes in (trusts in, clings to, relies on) Him shall not perish (come to destruction, be lost) but have eternal (everlasting) life. For God did not send the Son into the world in order to judge (to reject, to condemn, to pass sentence on) the world, but that the world might find salvation and be made safe and sound through Him.*

I'M SAVED! NOW WHAT?

The devil does not want us to really come to know God because he knows when we really know God, he will lose his lying influence over us.

2 Corinthians 4:4
> *"For the god of this world has blinded the unbelievers' minds [that they should not discern the truth], preventing them from seeing the illuminating light of the Gospel of the glory of Christ (the Messiah), Who is the Image and Likeness of God."*

One of the main reasons that Jesus came was to correct our view of Who God really is. When we see the life of Jesus, we are really seeing the Father. Jesus said, "When you see me, you see the Father". We know that Jesus did not come to be served but to serve and give His life as a ransom for many.

Jesus came preaching good news. He came healing and delivering people from the oppression of the devil. He came to set the captives free and to give them life and life more abundantly. This is the true nature of God! The true nature of God is to always heal, deliver, and bring people into life. The devil is come to steal, kill, and to destroy. We are blaming God for things that sin and the devil are to be blamed for. God is not out to destroy or condemn us but to save us!

The main way we get to know God and the true nature of God is through the word of God. If we are really going to come to know God and understand God's intentions for us, then we must do more than just casually read the Bible like we would read a fortune cookie. We must become a student of the word and we must renew our minds to the truth of the word.

Listen, we live in a very fallen world that is full of deception and constantly lying to us about Who God is and what His intention is toward us. Most are even telling us that there is no God at all, that we were created from slime or that we somehow created ourselves!

It's like the professor who asked his class at the beginning of the school year, how many believed in God. About half raised their hands. Then the professor told the ones who raised their hands, "Good, but by the end of the year you will not believe in God!" His mission was to convince them that there was no God. Sad to say our schools today are filled with fools and I didn't say this; the Bible says this.

Psalm 14:1
> *"The [empty-headed] fool has said in his heart, There is no God."*

Romans 1:21-23
> *"Because when they knew and recognized Him as God, they did not honor and glorify Him as God or give Him thanks. But instead they became futile and [c]godless in their thinking [with vain*

imaginings, foolish reasoning, and stupid speculations] and their senseless minds were darkened. Claiming to be wise, they became fools [professing to be smart, they made simpletons of themselves]. And by them the glory and majesty and excellence of the immortal God were exchanged for and represented by images, resembling mortal man and birds and beasts and reptiles."

The devil loves secular schools that teach evolution or teach that God is a figment of the imagination and that the very idea of creation is absolutely nonsense! They will often blame God for the cruelty of man-made religion so as to create doubt and unbelief in the hearts of people.

God is not the author of disasters or of cruel man-made religion. Much of this is a result of a fallen world and sin. God did not send His Son to punish us but to save us, not to condemn us but to give us eternal life. It is through understanding God's true nature and character that we will be set free from the lies of the devil.

CHAPTER 23

SATAN, THE GREAT CON ARTIST

When you take Scripture or text out of context, the only thing left is con. A con is someone that deceives by winning your confidence through twisted truth. Satan is the ultimate con artist. He actually uses the Bible by taking Scripture out of context to keep people bound in religion and condemnation. Satan is the ultimate con and deceiver, and he is the inventor of religion.

We see how Satan used God's word and twisted it in the very beginning to deceive Eve into eating from the only tree that God said don't eat from or you will die.

Genesis 3:1-4

"Now the serpent was more subtle than any beast of the field which the Lord God had made. And he said unto the woman,

> *Yea, hath God said, Ye shall not eat of every tree of the garden? And the woman said unto the serpent, We may eat of the fruit of the trees of the garden: But of the fruit of the tree which is in the midst of the garden, God hath said, Ye shall not eat of it, neither shall ye touch it, lest ye die. And the serpent said unto the woman, Ye shall not surely die."*

The devil does not want us to enjoy the abundant life nor the abundant blessings that God has so freely given us through Christ. The devil's only goal is to steal, to kill, and to destroy.

John 10:10
> *"The thief cometh not, but for to steal, and to kill, and to destroy: I am come that they might have life, and that they might have it more abundantly."*

The devil's mission is death. The Lord's mission is life. We must get this truth in our hearts to keep from deception. The devil wants to distract us from all the other trees in the garden that God said we could freely eat from, and eat from the tree that will only produce death. The trees in the garden, including the tree of life, represent God's grace, God's goodness, and God's abundant life and blessing.

How does the devil distract us and keep us bound? Again, it's often by taking God's word and twisting it to get us to believe that God is not really for us but against us, that God is really just out to get us. He gives us the impression that God is almost looking for a reason to toss us all into hell!

Satan uses religion, self achieving righteousness, and dead works to keep us bound in condemnation and away from walking in the abundant life that Christ came to lavish on us. Satan has cunningly accomplished this throughout church history by mixing the gospel of grace with law. He began this deception in the early church and it still by and large continues today.

Today we see more division, death, and condemnation than we do abundant life because of doctrines of devils.

1 Timothy 4

"Now the Spirit speaks expressly, that in the latter times some shall depart from the faith, giving heed to seducing spirits, and doctrines of devils."

It may shock you to know that the devil has his own preachers and teachers. In fact, many preach behind pulpits every Sunday! Just because someone has an education in theology and has the title preacher or even pastor, does not make him qualified or even a true minister of the gospel. Many are posing as ministers of righteousness, but they are not preaching faith righteousness which comes as a gift through the finished work of the cross. Instead, they are preaching self righteousness of religion, effort, and performance.

2 Corinthians 11:13-15
> *"For such are false apostles, deceitful workers, transforming themselves into the apostles of Christ. And no marvel; for Satan himself is transformed into an angel of light. Therefore it is no great thing if his ministers also be transformed as the ministers of righteousness; whose end shall be according to their works."*

We are not to be deceived by the so called professional ministers and priests with long robes. They are not all sent from God! Nor do they always represent the heart of God, the nature of God, or the will of God. Many do not even know what the New Covenant is or even where it's found in the Bible!

Satan uses people to speak his deception. Some are knowingly being used, but many are being used because of their ignorance of the gospel. This is why it's so vital for each of us to study the word for ourselves and ask the Holy Spirit, Who is our ultimate Teacher, to lead and guide us into all the truth. This is actually a big part of the New Covenant.

John 14:26
> *"But the Comforter, which is the Holy*

> *Ghost, whom the Father will send in my name, he shall teach you all things, and bring all things to your remembrance, whatsoever I have said unto you."*

1 John 2:27
> *"But the anointing which ye have received of him abides in you, and ye need not that any man teach you: but as the same anointing teaches you of all things, and is truth, and is no lie, and even as it hath taught you, ye shall abide in him."*

Now don't get me wrong – God has placed teachers and preachers in the church to instruct us. But ultimately, we all have the responsibly to get into the word for ourselves and ask the Holy Spirit to show us truth.

The devil has his own teachers preaching from the Bible, but they are often taking Scripture out of context. That produces bondage and death instead of freedom and life. The letter kills but the Spirit gives life.

Again, it is vital that each of us know the Word but that we are also led by the Spirit of truth as well.

2 Peter 2:1
> *"But there were false prophets also among the people, even as there shall be false teachers among you, who privily shall*

bring in damnable heresies, even denying the Lord that bought them, and bring upon themselves swift destruction."

The devil told Adam and Eve you will not die. He said God really knows that if you eat you will be like Him, being able to decide for yourself what is good and what is evil.

The devil's tactic is to pull us out of grace and into a "works and religious performance" way of doing and trying to earn and become what God has already made us to be and has already blessed us with.

The devil told Adam and Eve, "If you do this then you will become like God." Well, first of all, they were already created in the image of God. They didn't have to do anything to make this happen. Likewise, we are created in the righteousness of God through the new birth, and there is not one single other thing we have to do to make this happen or to maintain what God has already done!

If we allow the enemy to pull us out of grace and rest into religious performance, it will not produce life but death. This is why it's so vital for each of us to study the word for ourselves and ask the Holy Spirit, Who is our ultimate Teacher, to lead and guide us into all the truth.

CHAPTER 24

SAVED LOST, SAVED LOST?

Could a person ever sin their righteousness away? To better answer this question, maybe we should really ask another question. "Could you ever do enough good deeds before you were saved to change your sinful nature?" The answer is obviously, no! The only way you could ever be changed from a sinner to a saint is through faith in Christ in the new birth.

Romans 5:19

> *"For as by one man's disobedience many were made sinners, so by the obedience of one shall many be made righteous."*

We were made sinners because of Adam's disobedience, but through Christ's obedience, we who believe, are now made righteous. So, now that you are born again and righteous by nature, can your failures now ever make you unrighteous and sinful by nature? No!

You didn't do anything to make yourself righteous and you cannot do anything to now make yourself unrighteous. It's not what you did that made you righteous, it's what you believed!

Many denominations believe that you can be saved, lost and then saved again almost every other day or week based on your performance. This is simply not true. If you are under this belief system, you are involved in a religious, self righteousness, self effort maintenance program that is keeping you bound in a whole lot of fear, condemnation, and uncertainty. God does not want you to live in a continual state of fear, uncertainty or condemnation. God wants you to have a clean conscience. He wants you to be bold and always confident toward Him. It is never God's desire for us to walk in fear and condemnation or to shrink back from Him! Never! God finds no pleasure in those who shrink back from Him in fear.

Hebrews 10:19-23

"Having therefore, brethren, boldness to enter into the holiest by the blood of Jesus, By a new and living way, which he hath consecrated for us, through the veil, that is to say, his flesh; And having an high priest over the house of God; Let us draw near with a true heart in full

assurance of faith, having our hearts sprinkled from an evil conscience, and our bodies washed with pure water. Let us hold fast the profession of our faith without wavering, (for he is faithful that promised.)"

Hebrews 10:38
"Now the just shall live by faith: but if any man draw back, my soul shall have no pleasure in him."

God does not want you to look at your salvation as conditional, based on your own performance, but only based upon the obedience of Christ, the finished work of the cross, and God's own faithfulness to finish what He began in you.

Ephesians 1:13
"In whom ye also trusted, after that ye heard the word of truth, the gospel of your salvation: in whom also after that ye believed, ye were sealed with that holy Spirit of promise."

The Bible also teaches that once we are saved and then sealed with the Holy Ghost, (kind of like fruit in a mason jar is sealed!) Nothing from the outside can get in to contaminate or spoil what is fresh on the inside. Why would God save us and then seal us? There is only one word to describe God's action, and that's love. God loves us so much that He never wants anything to ever get between us and Him ever again.

Let me make this clear: although sin may not be able to unravel your righteousness, sin can still unravel your life. Sin can open up a door for the enemy to come in and wreak havoc in your physical life. Sin can destroy relationships, marriages, and health. Sin can make you miss out on the incredible plan that God has for your life. Cemeteries are filled with Christians who went to heaven, but never fulfilled God's perfect plan for their lives on earth because of sin. Sin can still have incredible earthly consequences for the believer in this life. Listen, fire does not care if you are righteous or unrighteous. If you stick your hand in fire, it will still burn you. Likewise, sin will still burn you if you play with it. So as the old expression goes, don't play with fire!

Romans 6:1-2
> *"What shall we say then? Shall we continue in sin, that grace may abound? God forbid. How shall we, that are dead to sin, live any longer therein?"*

We, as believers in Christ, are not saved by grace, sealed by the Holy Ghost and washed clean by the blood so that we could then be free to go out and play in the mud... No! We are saved by grace, sealed by the Holy Ghost and washed by the blood of Jesus so that we can now walk in a new loving, living relationship with God.

Galatians 6:22

> *"But now being made free from sin, and become servants to God, ye have your fruit unto holiness, and the end everlasting life."*

Now, let me reemphasize this important truth: when we are born into this world we were all born sinners; we all had a sinful nature before we even committed one sinful act. The Bible says that through Adam's disobedience all were made sinners. There was absolutely nothing that we ever had to do to make us unrighteous sinners. We were born into unrighteousness. We were born sinners. We inherited this fallen nature from Adam. The good news is just as we were all born sinners through one man's disobedience, we are all now made righteous through the obedience of One, and that One is Jesus. We did not have to do anything to make us righteous, because Jesus did it all at the cross. The only thing we have to do is to believe that Jesus did it all.

Romans 5:18-19

> *"Therefore as by the offence of one judgment came upon all men to condemnation; even so by the righteousness of one the free gift came upon all men unto justification of life.*

I'M SAVED! NOW WHAT?

> *For as by one man's disobedience many were made sinners, so by the obedience of one shall many be made righteous."*

When we said yes to Christ, something happened on the inside of us (that is in our spirit). The old man or old nature is taken away and a new nature is put into its place. This new nature is now holy and righteous and perfect.

2 Corinthians 5:17-18
> *"Therefore if any man be in Christ, he is a new creature: old things are passed away; behold, all things are become new. And all things are of God, who hath reconciled us to himself by Jesus Christ, and hath given to us the ministry of reconciliation."*

2 Corinthians 5:21
> *"For he hath made him to be sin for us, who knew no sin; that we might be made the righteousness of God in him."*

The main truth that we need to realize is this: just as there was not one sin that we had to commit to make us unrighteous sinners because we were all born sinners, likewise neither was there not one righteous deed that we could ever do to make us righteous or keep us righteous. Righteousness is a gift from God through the obedience of Jesus Christ. We must understand this truth to walk in the freedom

SAVED LOST, SAVED LOST?

that God wants us to walk in and reign in this life. The only thing we did to make us righteous was to believe in Jesus Christ and receive the free gift of God's grace and righteousness.

Romans 5:17
> "For if by one man's offence death reigned by one; much more they which receive abundance of grace and of the gift of righteousness shall reign in life by one, Jesus Christ."

The Amplified Bible expands this thought:
> "For if because of one man's trespass (lapse, offense) death reigned through that one, much more surely will those who receive [God's] overflowing grace (unmerited favor) and the free gift of righteousness [putting them into right standing with Himself] reign as kings in life through the one Man Jesus Christ (the Messiah, the Anointed One)."

About the Author

Rick Sarver is the co-pastor/teacher of The Church in the Hamptons in Myrtle Beach, SC. Rick is actively spreading the gospel also as both a dynamic speaker and a local business owner. His commitment to market place ministry has touched thousands as tourists come from all over the nation. He and his wife DeAnn make their home in Myrtle Beach, SC.

Follow Rick's blog at:

www.itsgrace.com

Made in the USA
Charleston, SC
29 December 2014